Avoiding Adversity

Avoiding
Adversity

---

*How Insiders and Outsiders can
Detect and Avoid Business Failure*

Bill Houston

David & Charles
Newton Abbot   London

British Library Cataloguing in Publication Data

Houston, Bill
  Avoiding adversity.
  1. Business firms. Crises. Financial
management
  I. Title
  658.1'5

  ISBN 0-7153-9403-7

Typeset by Typesetters (Birmingham) Ltd
Smethwick, West Midlands
and printed in Great Britain
by Billings Ltd, Worcester
for David & Charles Publishers plc
Brunel House Newton Abbot Devon

Contents

Introduction

Resolving a business crisis is similar to a retreating army taking up a sound defensive position. From what had been a position of withdrawal, disorganisation, desertion and despair must arise confidence, discipline, resource regrouping and a recovery plan.

A corporate crisis is seldom unexpected for those able to read the signals, and it has two causes:

- Commercial misjudgement which may range from an unwise acquisition to an inability to price correctly; both if allowed to continue will contaminate and sap strength from the healthy parts of the business.
- A failure to recognise the importance of the business cycle. For example, it might be sensible to borrow heavily on short-term money for a new venture at the start of a cycle; the same action taken at the end will put the company at grave risk of failure.

This book is written primarily for those managing a company rescue and gives a practical agenda for tackling the crisis. Part One deals with the work of turnround; Part Two with measures to strengthen the balance sheet and Part Three with a completely new approach to reducing fixed costs.

The book is also written for those who are connected with, or concerned about, the fate of a company; they may be bankers, shareholders, employees, trading partners, professionals or journalists. A company facing a crisis presents a picture of confusion and bravado to the outsider who knows something is wrong but finds it difficult to pinpoint the exact problem. The aim of Part Four is to assemble publicly available information and put it into the wider context so that people external to the company can make their own decision about a future relationship.

9

INTRODUCTION

Moving from offensive action to the defence is not easy and requires a change in command attitudes. An attacking general raised on the thrusting doctrines of Clausewitz may have difficulty switching to the subtleties of Sun Tzu – the Chinese military theoretician who lived around 500BC and whose doctrine guided Mao Tse Tung's guerrilla forces against those of the regular army.

So it is with commercial commanders. Aggressive builders of corporate empires are seldom able to face the more flexible and subtle style of defence needed to cope with a crisis. Conversely, few turnround specialists are comfortable with an offensive command when risks may put their balance sheet in jeopardy.

A new defensive commander, military or commercial, has only a short time to gain the confidence of subordinates and outsiders. Anyone taking on this role will need to pinpoint the prime weaknesses, move swiftly to put these right, then regain strength before moving back to the offensive. This book helps to gain the initiative.

Contents Guide

Part One explains the reasons for crisis management and the remedy which is to fund debt and reduce costs. *Trading out of difficulty on a weak balance sheet without major operating changes is not an option.*

There are five chapters which cover the process from analysis through to action.

- Chapter 1 examines the various reasons companies get into trouble and identifies each stage of the decline.
- Chapter 2 explains that commercial decisions should not be made in isolation from the business cycle, and the appropriate policies for each phase.
- Chapter 3 describes the recovery process in detail from the analysis and plan preparation through to implementation.
- Chapter 4 considers three examples of actual recoveries showing the procedures in practice.
- Chapter 5 covers some of the personal qualities needed to tackle this work and how to initiate the recovery process.

Part Two is concerned with protecting the balance sheet because many companies do not recognise a crisis until they risk running out of cash. After a major commercial misjudgement, if losses are allowed to accumulate and borrowed money is spent, the balance sheet is stripped of saleable assets. *The material in Chapters 6 to 11 cannot stop managements from dissipating the balance sheet but it can help conserve these values from an external threat.*

- Chapter 9 describes a strategy for investment at the closing stages of the business cycle.
- Chapter 10 examines the financing of fixed assets.
- Chapter 6 is concerned with the management of cash and preserving its value.

CONTENTS GUIDE

- Chapter 7 examines the best way to protect receivables which are the financial life-blood of a business.
- Chapter 8 warns of inventory obsolescence and modern methods of stock reduction.
- Chapter 11 considers ways of raising money after a company crisis.

Part Three introduces 'third generation' ideas for reducing line and staff costs without impairing effectiveness. In the past, a recession, or the onset of fierce competition, has forced management to make closures and cutbacks. Now these problems may be tackled by introducing new methods of cost reduction such as agency working, franchising and remote working.

- Chapter 12 describes third generation methods in a historical context and shows how cutting costs and creating individual economic independence can work together.
- Chapter 13 explains how franchising, a method of licensing, can be used to recover assets and reduce the fixed cost of employment.
- Chapter 14 introduces new ideas for converting fixed to variable costs through remote working. The chapter covers a wide range of staff functions that can be worked remotely, either through full-time employment or by previous employees launched on their new independent careers.
- Chapter 15 shows how working through agents can reduce the cost of representation and service while control is exercised through an agency agreement.

Part Four is specifically for those outside a company who have a trading, investment or lending relationship, and who want to assess for themselves the wisdom of the board's policies at different stages in the business cycle. While Chapter 16 can be read on its own, the reader will find a more complete understanding if this is read in conjunction with other parts of the book.

Finally there is a comprehensive range of appendices.

CONTENTS GUIDE

- Appendix 1 is for those who wish to know more about business cycles and shows how to trace their progression.
- Appendix 2 provides an agenda for disposing of companies and assets – a crucial part of a recovery programme.
- Appendix 3 is designed as an *aide-memoire* for negotiating long-term contracts that could prove burdensome.
- Appendix 4 provides examples of hedging currency and interest rate risks.
- Appendix 5 describes methods of measuring corporate solvency.
- Appendix 6 is a comparison of economic events of the twenties and thirties with those of the eighties.
- Appendix 7 sets out the principles behind franchising.
- Appendix 8 sets out the advantages of franchising.
- Appendix 9 is a case study showing the impact of franchising the branch operations of a company.
- Appendix 10 is a case history of Plant Hire Company and their analysis of the implications of franchising.
- Appendix 11 explains the reasons for Rank Xerox encouraging remote working.
- Appendix 12 describes the experience of remote working for F International and CPS.
- Appendix 13 describes agency working in the USA.
- Appendix 14 explains how the UK milk delivery industry converted employees to independence.

This is a 'hands-on book', involving not only the manager sorting out a crisis, but also the outsider who wants to continue a relationship with the company. Both are essential to the rescue because a business can only continue if there is a correctly based understanding between all the parties.

Business is a dynamic activity that is continually evolving. Third generation methods of fixed cost reduction are important new ways of meeting ever-growing competition.

PART ONE

GETTING OUT OF TROUBLE

How businesses get into financial trouble and how to take avoiding action

1

How People Get Into Trouble

Apart from a national crisis, it is generally through bad management and not 'bad luck' that companies get into trouble[1] and eventually suffer financial distress. The cause is usually a major commercial or financial misjudgement which has bled cash out of the business to the detriment of both profits and the balance sheet. People running corporations are often aggressive and ambitious individuals who find it difficult to admit their mistakes or to call in a fresh mind to remedy past errors.

There are many forms of misjudgement which crop up repeatedly as if people never learn from past mistakes. For example, things seemed to go wrong after the merger booms of the late twenties and early seventies; we now await the outcome of the eighties boom! Likewise, despite continuous warnings, some companies have not installed any financial accounting to give warning of cash difficulties between audits and are surprised when they run out of money.

Here are some of the more usual problems. They sound simple when shown singly but may be difficult to spot at the time because the company is often unaware, or unwilling to admit, that they exist.

- Being unaware of a problem usually means that the internal financial systems are not focussing on the critical

---

[1]Throughout this book 'trouble' is defined as a progressive deterioration of profit margins and net worth, almost invariably accompanied by increasing debt (in relation to equity), and regular below-the-line extraordinary items. If allowed to continue uncorrected the result will be insolvency. The chairman's statement will be revealing; it is unlikely to refer to the real problem, tending instead to concentrate on matters such as expansion through acquisitions and increasing sales.

issues; in some cases, the problems are even deliberately obscured! The experienced owner/manager invariably has at hand daily facts such as the bank position, orders in, sales out and the state of debtors.

- Inadequate attention to pricing – particularly in the latter inflationary stages of a business cycle.
- Overtrading (which is to expand at too fast a rate for the available cash flow) is often given as a cause for trouble. This occurs particularly at the start of a business cycle when orders are taken on slender margins quoted during the previous recession.
- The 'flywheel' effect is a variation on overtrading which occurs late in the business cycle. Huge sums of money may be borrowed on a small capital base with the expectation that the company can seek a quotation; this is the classic leveraged buy-out which has been widespread in the USA and to a lesser extent in Britain and Australia. Towards the end of a business cycle, with interest rates rising, a company needs to generate ever-increasing sales just to service the debt.

  One example was a medium-sized engineering company in the field of construction equipment that tried to expand on too small a capital base just to pay interest; the problems were compounded when it bought additional sales by making acquisitions on further borrowings - a classic mistake that almost always goes wrong.

- Reliance on a single customer is often a cause of trouble, particularly for smaller companies. There have been a number of examples when a business has been delighted to gain a large account, only to find that margins were squeezed unmercifully once the reliance was total. This is a difficult problem to resolve unless the customer can be persuaded that he needs the supplier.

- Unwise acquisitions are probably the quickest way of getting into trouble, particularly if made with borrowed money at the end of a business cycle. One notable example was a successful construction company; the chairman (a large shareholder) went against the advice of his board to merge with a highly leveraged house builder when the housing market had already peaked. Within weeks of completion, house prices started to tumble and assets could not be sold fast enough to fund the debt. It was only after many anxious days that the board saved the shareholders' investment.

- Understanding the state of the business cycle has been an important factor in the USA where it has been the custom to make loans on fixed interest. This made good sense during the twenties and thirties when the long-term trend in interest rates was down; it has made much less sense since 1950, with the progressive increase in inflationary expectations (see Appendix 1, Chart 7).

  The Savings and Loans Associations (S & Ls) had a tradition of lending to home buyers at fixed rates of interest until 1979 when the market rates for money rose rapidly; quoted mortgage rates increased but the S & Ls had committed a high proportion of their loan portfolio at fixed rates. The income from the Thrifts – as the S & Ls are known – declined from a surplus of $5.7bn in 1978 to a loss of $5.9bn in 1982. In 1988 they were reported to be running at a loss of $1bn a month. Currently over 40 per cent are technically insolvent with a net worth of 3 per cent or less than their assets.

- The business cycle will also affect contracts taken on at a fixed price when the costs are variable. This subject is described in more detail in Chapter 16.

- Make or buy decisions have a crucial effect on performance if not reversed by market changes. One important company in the garment trade created a worldwide business based on treating imported cloth from China. Competitors modified the process using a cheaper base material which undercut the market leader who responded by reducing prices thereby squeezing margins. The losses were written off as extraordinary items which progressively drained the balance sheet leaving nothing for the investors or creditors.

- A major diversification is often sought by management, who believe that their own pricing, negotiating and contracting skills are adequate for the new venture. One successful prefabrication building company accepted a diversified contract in an Arabian Gulf state without any previous experience of working in the area or on that type of contract; not surprisingly, the customer required a performance bond. The plan required the components to be shipped to the country for assembly on a site prepared by the local associate. The problems of working in a completely strange environment with major difficulties of collecting progress payments nearly forced the company into receivership. It was only saved by its traditional business.

- A major investment decision – in anticipation of a contract or a new source of business – has often been the cause of trouble; it is also very difficult to correct because the value of the plant in other hands is much less than the original installation. A medium-sized agricultural engineer with a strong balance sheet was subject to a bid and in defence decided to make a major investment in a grey-iron foundry when there was casting overcapacity. This was during a period of rapid change in the industry when lighter materials were being sought and the investment became increasingly uneconomical. The board, who controlled the business, could not bring themselves to acknowledge their mistake and the company eventually failed.

The cause of trouble is not only a poor commercial decision but often faulty timing. There have been four identifiable business cycles in the USA since World War II which are described in more detail in Chapter 12; getting these right is a major policy decision. For example, it is often sensible to borrow money at the beginning of a business cycle because the interest and capital repayments will be covered by increased cash flow. It is folly to be overborrowed at the end of a cycle because at some time sales will fall and interest charges rise; this enforces painful cutbacks and the sales of assets to pay off debt. Early warning of the important turning points is critical.

When things go wrong they do not happen all at once. The results of an unwise decision often take years to show and will only be detected by a careful analyst who will look for four stages.

HOW PEOPLE GET INTO TROUBLE

Stage 1 *Euphoria*

A new contract or deal announced by the board as being a major step forward is duly reported by the financial press. The next three or six months' results will stress the benefits, probably concentrating on some particular feature (such as increased volume), without dwelling on the likely reduced profit margin or greater borrowings.

Stage 2 *Conviction*

The performance of the company will have declined but the chairman's statement will emphasise the success of the board's policies. However, it is possible that managerial and financial resources are being siphoned from the profitable products to make up for losses in the new areas. The 'conviction' stage may take two or three years during which there is a progressive decline in profit margins and a series of small write-downs slowly reduce the net worth. The board may reinforce their policy by making more deals or acquisitions.

Stage 3 *Determination*

The stock price is likely to have fallen during Stage 2 and the register will show that the investing institutions are reducing their commitment despite efforts to explain the position to the financial community. The board will become less united and there may be changes. If the business is to be saved, the chairman or chief executive should be replaced. For investors this could be a major buying opportunity; experience shows that either the company will be subject to a bid or new management will be brought in.

Stage 4 *Termination*

This is the saddest phase when management exhausts every source of cash to keep the business going. The investors may be lucky if there is a take-over bid, but only a brave buyer would take on a company that is excessively borrowed after pledging every available asset.

Unquestionably, some managers have successfully taken aggressive risks to improve earnings to the advantage of the company and shareholders. Difficulties arise when the executives are so committed to an unsound course that they fail to realise the potential disaster.

2

Management Style and the Business Cycle

The counterpoint to a management crisis (described in Chapter 1) is a financial crisis engendered (unwittingly) by politicians. It is possible to deal with each event in isolation but much more difficult when they occur together. The purpose of this chapter is to describe how the stages in the business cycle should affect commercial and investment decisions.

A financial crisis occurs when a rise in interest rates makes it intolerable to hold onto debt and there is a scramble for liquidity which further forces up the cost of money. Since World War II business cycles have been dependent upon the rise and fall of interest rates in the USA and there have been at least four such cycles since 1950, each one being more pronounced. The analysis, described in more detail in Appendix 1, shows that around every seven years there is a surge in inflation followed by a rise in short–term interest to dampen the economy. When the short-term rates rise beyond the long-term rates of interest, there follows a recession which has increased in intensity. The end of the last cycle was in 1980.

Business cycles tend to divide into at least three stages: coming out of a recession; the mid-term; then inflation and beyond. The third is the most exciting and potentially the most dangerous.

Stage 1 *Coming Out of Recession*
There are five or six years of growth ahead as politicians use every incentive to encourage expansion and increase employment. Interest rates will be low and favourable long-term loans or leasing arrangements may be negotiated with banks or finance houses. Real estate and equities are usually

a sound investment and low commodity prices will encourage long–term contracts for the supply of raw materials. A number of companies fail through overtrading at this part of the cycle and steps should therefore be taken to protect receivables. It would be wise to review prices quoted during the previous recession.

One of the most important investments will be management. The subtle and flexible management style, that has served the company safely during the recession and left a strong balance sheet, may be inadequate for Stage 2. Managers who will do well in the growth phase will be determined, aggressive people committed to action.

Stage 2 *The Mid-Term*
When the ambitious plans laid during Stage 1 materialise, the business will prosper from the contracts negotiated earlier. As Stage 2 continues, it would be sensible to make acquisitions provided they can later be funded by rights issues. One excellent strategy is to generate new divisions that can be split from the parent and hived off into separately quoted companies.

Towards the end of Stage 2 inflation will influence prices and interest rates but costs will be under control through the long-term purchase contracts negotiated earlier. Stage 2 is a good time to invest in productivity to keep down costs as employment expenses increase. The strong cash flow from these measures should be used for paying off debt as interest rates become positive (ie higher than the rate of inflation).

Stage 3 *Inflation and Beyond*
This is the most difficult stage to manage because timing will be affected by outside events such as a US presidential election. There will be an excess of credit at the end of the cycle; surplus funds can either be invested into financial assets (as in 1929 and 1987) or physical assets like commodities (as in 1980). In each case a rapid rise is followed by a dramatic crash.

Stage 3 is potentially the most dangerous for companies caught with a weak balance sheet and high secured borrowings. There will be warnings, however, because Stage 3 can be divided into three phases: inflation, financial crisis and decline.

Phase A *Inflation*

Post-war business cycles have ended in an inflationary spurt as consumers borrow to keep up spending levels. Extra debt has to be paid for by higher interest charges and the debt-pile accumulates. The extra demand also bids up wages and raw materials, fuelling inflation. Business is good during this phase and the extra cash should be applied to pay off debt. Now is the time to make contingency plans to reduce costs. (Part Three describes new ways of cutting expenditure without harming the business.)

Phase B *Financial Crisis*

The crisis is triggered by the government's worry that inflation is getting out of hand; their remedy is to increase short-term interest rates which forces overborrowed businesses and people into loss. Borrowings can be reduced either through repayment or repudiation (which is the same as failure). Both are ominous. Forced repayment means that assets need to be sold quickly, so driving down prices; repudiation means that a tranche of credit is destroyed and most of the people expecting payment lose their money. There are wide repercussions. The huge demand for money forces interest rates to 'spike', the worst point in the crisis.

Phase C *Decline*

The authorities reduce interest rates as soon as possible to lessen chaos, as happened in late 1929 and in 1981. However, much damage occurs and overborrowed companies are reluctant to take on more credit, so slowing down the trading process. As activity declines so does government revenue, and the Treasury dares not increase its own borrowing for fear of tipping even more companies into receivership.

In 1931, so concerned was the British Government that it actually cut the pay of all state employees by 15 per cent, and increased taxes in order to balance the budget. The US also cut federal costs severely when, as part of the New Deal,

President Roosevelt reduced salaries of federal employees and veterans' entitlements by $500m and the defence budget was cut by nearly 30 per cent.

Management Agenda

The cover plan prepared in Phase A concentrates on protecting the value of the balance sheet and reducing costs, to be covered in Parts Two and Three respectively. The board agenda should include the following items:

- Debt is the most dangerous liability during a crisis and should be paid off during Phase A when assets such as real estate will fetch a good value. Unwanted subsidiaries should also fetch a good price either sold as a management buy-out or to a third party. See Appendix 2 for hints on selling assets.
- Cash is 'king' during a recession. Take appropriate steps to protect its value, see Chapter 6.
- Protect cash flow by taking measures to ensure that receivables are collected, see Chapter 7.
- Inventory ages rapidly and will need to be written down if slow-moving through a fall in sales, or obsolete due to product changes. A cash shortage in good for spares businesses as people make their equipment last longer, see Chapter 8.
- Investments will decline during a financial crisis and should be liquidated apart from key core holdings, see Chapter 9.
- Long-term liabilities such as property leases, purchase agreements and labour contracts will become onerous, hindering adjustment to declining sales and increased competition. Before taking professional advice on these matters, look through Appendix 3.
- Reduce fixed costs to withstand a reduction in sales volume and slimmer margins. The objective is to lower the break-even point by converting fixed into variable costs. Reducing expenses is a lengthy business requiring analysis and negotiation and should be undertaken as early as possible, see Part Three.
- Product development and marketing will become even

more important during a recession as competition forces innovation. Consider methods of hiring skills set out in Chapter 14.

- Recast the budget to allow for a drop in volume/ margins of up to 25 per cent over a five-year period. There was a drop in value of American manufactured goods of 50 per cent from 1929 to 1934.

Do not be alarmed by these measures – they may not need to be implemented – but be prepared for the worst. All the events described in Stage 3 have occurred in previous cycles and may not happen again. Politicians may indeed have learned the secret of organising perpetual growth, but it would be unwise to bank on it!

3

Getting Out of Trouble

It is now possible to assemble several strands of information to look back in time and discover the reason why a company has found itself in trouble.

In matters of turnround the past is a guide to future action and this chapter is written both for present management and those to take command. Each should start with a review of the past.

- Make a five-year analysis of the available data to show the major changes in margins, borrowings, etc. This work will be much more revealing if amplified by using the agencies described in Appendix 5.
- Compare the data with the published press and company statements to see the relationship between the facts and the perceived situation within the company.
- Pinpoint the misjudgement that caused the trouble and try to interpret the way in which performance has been affected.
- Discern the degree of crisis and the potential involvement of anyone coming in to take charge.
- Outline a plan – to be confirmed from greater knowledge.

Any plan needs two essential components for a recovery. Their application will depend upon the severity of the crisis:

- Funding debt through the disposal of assets.
- Reducing costs.

You cannot trade out of trouble on a weak balance sheet without making major operating changes.

When things have gone badly wrong, a good rescue plan will result in the following:

- Reduced sales as unprofitable products or companies go.
- Improved margins from the reduction of costs.
- Reduced debt through the disposal of assets.
- An improved output per employee.
- An extraordinary write-down of assets to a realistic valuation.

The task confronting a turnround manager varies enormously from a mild application of discipline to dealing with an outright panic. For the purpose of this chapter the worst case is assumed where the manager has to initiate stringent and rapid cash controls before proceeding to the remedial stage.

The two following sections are the outcome of several years of turnround experience, drawing together many management disciplines. For a more complete view of the techniques, look through the business sections of libraries and bookshops; titles for your consideration should include Stuart Slatter's *Corporate Recovery*.

First Aid
The first moves are vital. Anybody taking control of an ailing business must assume that things have gone badly wrong; this implies financial haemorrhage which, if not corrected, will be terminal. There are at least five main areas of attack:

- Stop all cheques and purchases over a certain level – say £1,000 – unless sanctioned by the financial manager/team leader. This measure will be hotly debated but needs to be accepted by the operating managers until more information is available about the solvency of the business.
- Stop recruitment, new liabilities and other commitments unless these are confirmed by the new leader. In addition, scrutinise any major item of expenditure (ordered, but not delivered) and expenses such as foreign travel.
- Scrutinise the overdue sales ledger for accounts that can be collected quickly. When things have gone wrong, payments will have been delayed over credit-note disputes which should be resolved rapidly.

- Scour the inventory for surplus items that are readily saleable.
- Recast the cash-flow statement, inform the bank of the position and place a senior financial manager with an 'iron fist' in charge of cash control. It may be necessary to negotiate payment schedules with certain vociferous accounts to prevent them forming a committee of creditors. At all times it is essential to keep good lines of communication with the clearing bank.

If there is little or no possibility of generating enough cash to pay the creditors (and contingent liabilities) as they fall due, the company is in grave danger of trading while insolvent. Do not prevaricate. Advise the board immediately to take legal opinion on the correct approach towards the bank and the other creditors.

Recovery Action

Once the financial tourniquet has been successfully applied, the next step is to work out a recovery plan to be achieved in conjunction with management groups. The aim is to cut costs and fund debt through asset disposal. This is a somewhat involved process outside normal management duties but is essential to the learning and revival process. To use stock-market jargon, the task is to separate the 'holds' from the 'sells'. Holds are those activities, products, companies or divisions that are essential to the future of the business. The sells are those that can be converted into cash, or closed to generate funds and reduce costs. As already described, unwinding the sells almost invariably means a write-down of assets.

Consider the process in five stages:

- Stage 1   Deciding upon the framework.
- Stage 2   Going about the analysis.
- Stage 3   Testing the findings.
- Stage 4   Preparing the survival plan.
- Stage 5   Sorting out the organisation.

This sounds formidable, representing much hard work. However, persevere because three things will be detected, if they are not immediately apparent.

- The original misjudgement(s) that started the trouble.
- The almost invariable Pareto relationship or 80/20 rule.
- The time available for action.

Some of the likely misjudgements were described in Chapter 1 and most problems are variations on a theme. The Pareto relationship implies that 80 per cent of profits derive from 20 per cent of the products. The analysis is made simpler if these, or other patterns, can be recognised.

The further factor is timing. Everyone in the business will know that changes will take place and it is a period of great uncertainty when some of the best people will be tempted to leave. To avoid this, involve many of the potential high-fliers in the management decision groups.

The leader will be under scrutiny from shareholders, bankers, creditors and customers, as well as the employees. A recovery team leader starts with considerable goodwill but there will be understandable apprehension about the future (and not a little suspicion). There is no time to waste.

Stage 1   Deciding Upon the Framework
There will be parts of the business that will be obvious 'holds' and 'sells', which do not need a thorough examination to decide their future. There will also be those areas of unknown or doubtful profitability to be tackled by the management groups.

Before acting, consider the following principles:

- Confine the working parties to senior people whose knowledge and ability will almost certainly qualify them for a continuing place in the company. The work should be kept confidential.
- Consider the inclusion of outside specialists in turnround work. Their value lies in being able to challenge accepted practices.
- Include an arbitration group to settle differences of interpretation.

- Set a firm timetable for all four stages of the programme and ensure that one person, for example the company secretary or chief accountant, takes the minutes of the major meetings and acts as the progress chaser.

Stage 2   Going About the Analysis

Where the 'holds' or 'sells' are not clearly defined, the analysis must be applied to each operating division. Separate all revenues, expenses and assets and allocate these according to an agreed number of products or activities. Most accounting systems only allocate the prime cost of labour and materials, leaving the remainder of the expenses as general overheads. Assets are not normally allocated to products. The working parties will need to work out new costing and reporting systems that should then form part of the management accounts. The following guidelines should be adapted to suit individual cases:

Part 1   Cost Allocation

The aim is to allocate all expenses by an agreed number of product lines. Adapt Fig. 1 as a framework for recording data.

Part 2   Asset Allocation

The next step is to divide the assets between the 'holds' and the 'sells'. Some assets are used for different products or activities, and the allocation needs to be known before deciding on what must be kept and what can be sold. Adapt Fig. 2 for data collection.

Stage 3   Testing the Findings

The analysis will throw up areas of dispute and these will need to be resolved before drawing up the action plan. The main disagreements will probably concern expense allocations (particularly by people responsible for new or pet projects). These differences will need to be sorted out by the arbitration group set up during Stage 1. It is very important that the borderline issues are decided before moving to the next stage to avoid delaying the entire project.

Product Line Profitability
£m or $m

Sales and expense headings	Product groups						Total
	1	2	3	4	5	6	
Sales (1a)							
less							
Prime cost (1c)							
Contribution							
less overheads							
Transaction costs (1d)							
Value costs (1e)							
Occupational costs (1f)							
Capital costs (1g)							
General costs							
Profit before taxes							

1a Define the products or activities into up to 10 groups recognisable throughout the business.

1b Take a representative accounting period that acknowledges recent changes.

1c Allocate direct expenses, bought-in material and people including employment costs.

1d Allocate the transaction costs – those that are directly applicable to transacting an order. The departments concerned may include the sales office, production control, engineering (if made to order), shipping, sales ledger or accounts. Work out the number of orders transacted for each product group and divide the costs.

1e The next overhead sector may be defined as the value group – the expenses allocated by individuals who have a direct responsibility for spending. The departments might include marketing, development, public relations, production overheads, quality control, purchasing and inventory control. This method, in practice, has proved to be both revealing (to the individuals concerned) and accurate in allocating cost centres particularly when some products attract undue complexities.

1f The occupancy group of expenses will include those related to housing people. This heading will cover heating, lighting, rent, rates and insurances.

1g Capital items attract depreciation, interest power and maintenance; these should be allocated by the sales volume generated by the asset.

Fig. 1 Sample cost allocation sheet

Product Line Asset Distribution
£m or $m

Asset headings	Product groups						Total
	1	2	3	4	5	6	
Property (2a)							
Plant (2b)							
Investments (2c)							
Receivables (2d)							
Inventory (2e, 2f)							
Creditors (2f)							
Cash/borrowings (2g)							

Total assets

2a Allocate factory and commercial property on the same basis as 1f.

2b Allocate the plant values on the same basis as 1g.

2c It will not be possible to assign product groups to investments unless they relate to group strategy.

2d The major accounts are the most important (usually 80 per cent of sales go to 20 per cent of customers); these need to be divided into product groups. Other debtors can be divided by personal knowledge.

2e Inventory valuation and allocation could be complicated by the accounting systems generally available. Finished stock will be simple but the working parties may have to design novel systems of costing before the work-in-progress can be allocated.

2f Allocate trade creditors by finished stock. Other creditors can be allocated as appropriate, for example, people costs.

2g The difference of cash and borrowings is divided by product volume.

Fig. 2 Sample asset allocation sheet.

Stage 4   Preparing the Survival Plan
The completed lists of holds and sells can now be scrutinised
to achieve improved performance and a positive cash flow.
The next step is to work out an individual strategy.

- Holds. These represent the future of the business and
  first-aid investment may be needed to ensure their
  immediate continuity and competitiveness. Investment
  for growth comes after generating a positive cash flow.
- Sells. Assemble the assets – be these companies, plant,
  real estate or working capital – in a form that will attract
  buyers. Each will require a separate approach; consult
  Appendix 2 for a detailed strategy.

Aide-memoire for the disposal programme:
- List all the sells by size of assets. These will invariably
  include items that are unsaleable or are worthless which
  should be 'junked' quickly. There may, however, be
  overstocked items of obsolete lines that might be completed and sold for well above scrap value in a different
  market.
- Assemble small disposal teams, each including a manager
  who has knowledge of the asset to be sold (this person's
  redundancy or redeployment arrangements should have
  been agreed in advance – few people have a clear
  mind when their future is uncertain). Work from the
  largest asset and categorise them into the three groupings
  described below.
- Consider carefully the content and timing of any an-
  nouncement. Piecemeal revelations of future plans can be
  very unsettling particularly when families hear of a redundancy programme before the employees. The matter is
  further complicated with international companies because
  of time differences and rapid means of communication.

Arrange the assets in three categories:

Category 1   Management Buy-out
A purchase by the present management has the advantage
of confidentiality and has the merit of the least disturbance

to customers and employees. As this is a friendly disposal, it may be necessary to augment the asset to include other products. If the package is in the form of a company, consider including a level of debt acceptable to the purchaser. If a buy-out is not possible, consider outside purchasers.

Category 2   Asset or Activity Sales

A redundant product may have plant or equipment that can produce items of value in other hands. It is often possible for an attractive package to be put together that will provide continuing employment for operators and managers. Where a finished product or work-in-progress is independent from its associated plant, this should be sold separately. It is sometimes possible to negotiate attractive prices from competitors.

Category 3   Closure

This alternative never retains jobs but it is possible for certain individuals to be redeployed when the assets are sold.

Stage 5   *Sorting Out the Organisation*

A well-constructed recovery programme is an opportunity to purge an organisation that was facing in too many directions. Ridding companies of loss-making products or activities releases people into constructive work that is not in perpetual crisis. The impact on the business is cathartic.

These are some guidelines which can be adapted to any business:

- Reconstruct from the bottom up so that as many tiers of management as possible are removed between the general manager and the individual operative.
- Promote from within wherever possible. A recovery plan is a wonderful way of encouraging and training good people who were 'locked in' to the previous structure.
- Review make or buy decisions once the loss-making products or activities have been sold. It may be possible to focus operations more precisely and bring in specialised machinery.
- Widen the purchasing function to include control over

the inventory; its status could be raised further when 'Just In Time' (JIT) methods described in Chapter 8 are introduced. One of the first tasks will be to review present sources, costs and quality of supplies.

- Introduce a top-level forum where major innovations such as JIT or quality-control systems can be initiated. An initial task of the group should be an investigation into the level of credit note requests – invariably a result of crisis management.
- Review customer files to revive sales in neglected accounts. This is most efficiently implemented by producing an account analysis categorising potential and actual customers. There is usually a rich vein of knowledge that can be used to sharpen the selling effort in the most rewarding areas; this knowledge should also be applied to a revision of prices and discounts.
- Reconsider distribution to take into account small value orders. A company in trouble tends to accept a large number of small orders on the principle that margins are higher. This is almost always a fallacy. There is a minimum cost for handling a credit order; small value purchases should be directed towards other means of distribution.
- Adapt management accounts so that they are intelligible and can be acted upon by middle management. One of the first tasks of the management team will be to produce a new budget.
- Tighten the links between development and marketing in order to accelerate innovation. This action will help retain the loyalty of customers, strained during periods of crisis and rapid change.

4

Recovery in Action

Examples of Manufacturing and Service Companies Getting Out of Trouble

The message of the previous chapters is that it is only possible to get out of a financial mess by reducing costs and selling assets to fund debt; any attempt to trade out of trouble without major operational changes only drains resources from areas that are still healthy. This dictum was well covered by Irving Sprague in his book *Bailout*. Sprague was chairman of the Federal Deposit Insurance Corporation (FDIC) during the rescue of Continental Illinois. The book explains that in a bank rescue the FDIC's executives sterilise the non-performing loans, then attract bids for the healthy parts of the loan portfolio.

The rescue of a trading company follows precisely the same process. First analyse the position, next divide the holds from the sells, then make disposals so that the healthy parts survive.

This chapter describes the rescue of three companies that needed an external influence to trigger recovery. Their trades are diverse as are the solutions and for obvious reasons their location is disguised. They have been deliberately chosen for their size; sales of around £10m represents a small private company or subsidiary of a group.

Example A   Specialist Pressure Hose and Fitting Manufacturer

A is a subsidiary of a US parent engaged in the manufacture of high-pressure hydraulic hose and fittings based in Chicago. The company sells to original equipment manufacturers (OEMs) making machine tools and mobile equipment and one of the larger accounts is a sister subsidiary. There is

37

Year	1	2	3
Sales in $m	10.5	11.0	11.5
Profit before taxes $,000s	500	150	(100)

Balance sheet for year 3 $m

Leasehold premises		0.6	
Plant and equipment		2.0	
Inventory	2.5		
Receivables	1.9		
Cash	0.3		
less Creditors	2.6		
Borrowings	1.0		
Net current assets		1.1	
Net assets		3.7	

Fig. 3   Abbreviated accounts and balance sheet

also a growing business to distributors serving the secondary market. The company's performance is poor with almost flat sales over a three-year period; the abbreviated accounts are shown in Fig 3 with the balance sheet for year 3.

The parent company was concerned about the performance and formed a small working party consisting of A's president with a team from head office. There was no obvious commercial misjudgement although the team believed that A might be at a disadvantage; it was understood that competitors were purchasing machined fittings while A still had a sizeable machine shop and tool room. The team decided to conduct a product and asset analysis similar to that described in Chapter 3 with the results shown in Fig 4.

Product groups	Pressure hose	Fittings	Attachment	Total
Sales $m	3.5	7.0	1.0	11.5
Direct cost	0.7	3.5	0.4	4.6
Contribution	2.8	3.5	0.6	6.9
Overhead expenses	2.1	4.5	0.4	7.0
Profit before taxes	0.7	(1.0)	0.2	(0.1)
Asset distribution $m				
Fixed assets	0.4	2.0	0.2	2.6
Working capital	0.3	0.6	0.2	1.1
People employed	44	140	13	197

Fig. 4 Product and asset analysis

The analysis supported the suspicion that the production of fittings was the main culprit and tied up by far the largest value of assets (the Pareto in this case was that the loss was coming from 60 per cent of the sales and 70 per cent of the assets). Time in this case was not an important factor.

The obvious remedy would be to close the machine shop, buy in the components and move to smaller premises. This, however, was not appropriate because the plant and tooling was dedicated to fitting production and was needed for future supply. The manufacturers of the plant were consulted and confirmed that the equipment might be able to produce pneumatic fittings with some additional outlay for tooling. There were a number of sub-contract machine shops in the area, of which two expressed an interest in taking on the plant and supplying components, however, they could not afford the purchase price even at the written-down value.

The Solution

It was agreed that one of the sub-contractors buy the plant at the written-down price over a five-year period, to be paid by supplying the fittings at an agreed works cost. It was calculated that over the period the difference between the works cost and market price would pay for the plant.

A would keep title to the plant until it was paid for in fitting supplies and there was a strict schedule of thirty-day payment terms to maintain the supplier's cash flow. The most satisfactory part of the agreement was the re-employment of most of the fitters and operators who knew the work intimately; compensation terms were agreed as was the transfer of pension funds.

Note This was one case where it was not necessary to make a major asset write-down at the start. The balance sheet would be changed over the five years with the sales of plant being compensated by an increase in cash from the added margins on sales (less tax).

Example B   Diversified Jobbing Shop

B was bought by a larger group in the 'merger mania' of the eighties. It was an odd choice for an acquisition but one of the more aggressive managers of the bidding company believed that there were possibilities for expansion and he was appointed chief executive. The company, located in the north of England, had started as an engineering support business from which it had developed a line of material-handling machinery for the mining industry.

Subsequently the new manager embarked on two diversifications; one was sub-contract work for a sophisticated mechanical-handling project including computerised control of storage. The other was a specialist machining contract involving very high standards of work for a Japanese principal. The results for the latest three years and the balance sheet for the third are set out in Fig 5.

Year	1	2	3
Sales £m	7.5	8.0	10.5
Profit before tax £000s	650	700	800

Balance sheet for year 3 £m		As audited	Adjusted
Property		2.3	2.3
Plant and machinery		2.5	2.5
Inventory	2.1		0.7
Receivables	3.5		2.0
Cash	–		
less Creditors	2.6		2.6
Borrowings	2.3		2.3
Net current assets		0.7	(2.2)
Long-term loan		(2.0)	(2.0)
Net assets		3.5	0.6

Fig. 5   Abbreviated accounts and balance sheet

On the face of it, the company was doing well with rising sales and profits. However, the cash flow was negative and the parent company was being asked to provide even more resources. It was decided that before more loans were made available the internal audit team from head office be asked to make some checks. This was resisted by the confident management team but they were invited to participate in what was, after all, a routine check. The results were interesting (see Fig 6) especially as the figures were based on an audit carried out by an international firm of accountants.

Activities	Mechanical handling	Local contract	Machining work	Special contract	Total
Sales £m	2.2	1.8	4.5	2.0	10.5
Direct costs	1.1	1.1	2.3	1.5	6.0
Contribution	1.1	0.7	2.2	0.5	4.5
less overheads	0.5	0.6	2.0	0.6	3.7
Profit before tax	0.6	0.1	0.2	(0.1)	0.8
Asset allocation					
Fixed assets	0.8	0.3	2.8	0.9	4.8
Current assets	1.3	0.2	2.8	1.3	5.6
Current creditors	0.7	0.3	2.6	1.3	4.9
Term Loan			2.0		2.0

Fig. 6   Internal audit team's findings

The management was surprised by the Pareto relationship on the traditional mechanical-handling business, believing it to be a 'yesterday' product as they called it. They were comforted by the notion that they only needed to chase up payment for the machining contract, tighten up somewhat on the new mechanical-handling work and all would be well. It was not to be.

The management believed that they had a number of concessions on the machining contract which had not been confirmed and their customer had been too polite to repudiate the invoices. This meant a write-down of £1.5m from the receivables and a loss for the machining business of £1.3m. A further blow was the contractual state of the mechanical-handling project. What appeared to be an asset of £1.1m actually became a negative value of £0.3m, ie this amount of labour and materials was needed to bring it up to value. This meant a write-down of £1.4m from work-in-progress which was added to the previous loss of £0.1m. The amended balance sheet had a net worth of £0.6m.

The Solution

The business was hardly worth keeping and with its past history it would have been difficult to sell to another manufacturer. The only practical solution was to offer the company to the management as a buy-out (they still believed the write-down was only bad luck). In the end a price of £0.3m was agreed with the removal of the bank guarantee from the parent.

Note This was a good little business before the diversifications became disastrous. It was fortunate for the parent company that the management still had the self-confidence to sell themselves to a new backer.

Example C   Office Equipment Distributor

C was an independent office equipment distributor in Melbourne, Australia, that also carried an imported line of printing machines which it was required to service. In addition, the business was the sole distributor for a verification machine which it sold to large retail accounts.

Performance had been patchy; a number of new ventures had been tried including hi-fi equipment, but these had come to nothing and had to be sold at a loss. The last three-year abbreviated accounts show a static position with declining margins, see Fig 7.

Year	1	2	3
Sales A$m	5.0	5.2	5.4
Profit before tax A$›000s	200	50	–
Balance sheet for year 3 A$m			
Fixed assets		1.5	
Inventory	1.0		
Receivables	1.2		
Cash	–		
less Creditors	1.4		
Borrowings	1.5		
Net current assets		(1.0)	
Net assets		0.5	

Fig. 7   Abbreviated accounts and balance sheet

RECOVERY IN ACTION

Some of the shareholders were in the trade and knew that C's performance was not due to bad luck. The energetic chief executive was trying to do too much at once and was encouraged to work with a small team appointed by the shareholders. The group first carried out an activity analysis, see Fig 8.

Activity	Office	Printing	Verifier	Total
Sales A$m	0.8	3.0	1.6	5.4
Prime cost	0.5	1.8	0.6	2.9
Contribution	0.3	1.2	1.0	2.5
less overheads	0.3	1.8	0.4	2.5
Profit before taxes	–	(0.6)	0.6	–
Asset distribution				
Fixed assets	0.5	0.8	0.2	1.5
Net current assets	0.2	(1.5)	0.3	(1.0)

Fig. 8   Activity analysis

The team correctly concluded that there was little point in attempting to increase sales of the printing machine to the break-even point of A$4.5m against stiff competition. They also discovered that the office equipment customers were all small, reflecting the limited ability to give discounts. The team's greatest encouragement was to learn that there was considerable potential for the verifier which had been swamped by the other products.

The Solution
With the agreement of the suppliers, other distributors were appointed to carry the office equipment and printer products and the inventory was transferred with some loss. This left the verifier which could be sold from smaller premises. Fortunately many of the staff were taken on by the new distributors which left a small team under the chief executive. After all the transactions and costs, the company was left with little debt and a positive cash flow.

Note   This is a classic recovery where no great harm was done by the misjudgement to diversify, except mounting borrowings. The company was lucky to have a sound product and saleable assets to fund the debt.

5

Initiating Recovery

This book assumes that someone other than the present chief executive is likely to be needed to lead a corporate recovery. It is possible, but unlikely, that a leader who had presided over a declining performance would have the clarity of mind to recognise – and then rectify – their own past mistakes.

Recovery action may come from within the company, if the non-executive directors have sufficient strength. If not, the banks, concerned about the safety of their loans, or shareholders, worried about a decline in performance, may initiate the necessary moves to appoint a new leader. Whatever the trigger, the individual selected is at the start of a vigorous learning curve.

The manager would be wise to begin with an outline plan (described in Chapter 3 as a 'moving hypothesis') which can be developed as more information becomes available. The plan takes on a much sharper focus when the person appointed starts work within the business. Speed is essential as rumours about the likely changes will spread quickly and there is a danger that the best people will leave. Chapter 3 allows around three months from the start of the investigation to implementation.

Someone responsible for turning round a company has the singular privilege of rescue and then rebirth. Those who wish to develop a taste for turnround work might consider the following skills:

- *Curiosity* Some turnround specialists may know the business they are called upon to rescue, most do not. It is a tremendous help to have an enquiring mind.

- *Numeracy* A respect and facility for accountancy is essential although it is not necessary to be qualified. If the financial function is weak, it is vital that the person responsible is either replaced or supported from day one.

- *Clarity*   Any commander needs to have very clear objectives for the short and medium term and to be single-minded in their attainment. Most people dislike being 'hatchet men' but at times it is essential to make changes for the good of the business as a whole.

- *Involvement*   If the turnround leader is a newcomer to the business – and most are – they will have to rely heavily on existing people for local knowledge; many managers have a good feel for what is wrong and will respond enthusiastically to a 'new broom'. The investigating committees proposed in Chapter 3 are an ideal vehicle for retaining the interest and commitment of managers.

- *Leadership*   Once a plan has been agreed and announced, a good leader will see and be seen around the company explaining the present policies and how they are expected to work. A turnround represents a period of rapid change and the person responsible will be one of the few individuals who has reason for confidence even if the final outcome is not clear.

- *Background*   Most turnround specialists come from a background of general management with an experience of several industries; a period as an executive with an acquisitive conglomerate is also a good apprenticeship. Supplemental reading from turnround case studies is beneficial, as are the biographies of business, military and political leaders. Remember Bismarck's dictum that whereas other people learned from their own mistakes, he learned by reading about other people's errors!

- *Continuity*   The successful continuation of a business should be the aim of the competent turnround leader whether that person remains in command or not. In other words, *the ultimate aim is to lead by creating the setting for others to be successful.*

PART TWO

PROTECTING THE BALANCE SHEET

Preserving asset values is the surest way of not running out of cash

6
Retaining the Value of Cash

There is not too much concern for the security of cash during the first two stages of a business cycle (as defined in Chapter 2) except possible loss due to currency exchange. The third stage is a different matter and can be dangerous and destabalising. Whenever the authorities have applied pressure to quell inflation, there has been a rapid rise in interest rates which has forced overborrowed companies into insolvency. Appendix 1 describes the history of the US cycles in more detail.

This chapter has five sections. Those relating to the use of financial futures and options are reprinted by permission of the London International Financial Futures Exchange Limited (LIFFE):

- Risks to cash.
- Security of deposits.
- Protection against currency exchange risks.
- Introduction to financial futures and options.
- Hedging techniques.

Risks to Cash

The three main risks concern the loss of deposits through insolvency, currency exchange risks and the possibility of international default.

Loss through Insolvency
It is now rare for depositors to lose their money. In both Britain and the USA, the central banks have taken considerable pains to support the deposit base either through the 'lifeboat' operations in Britain or federal-backed insurance

49

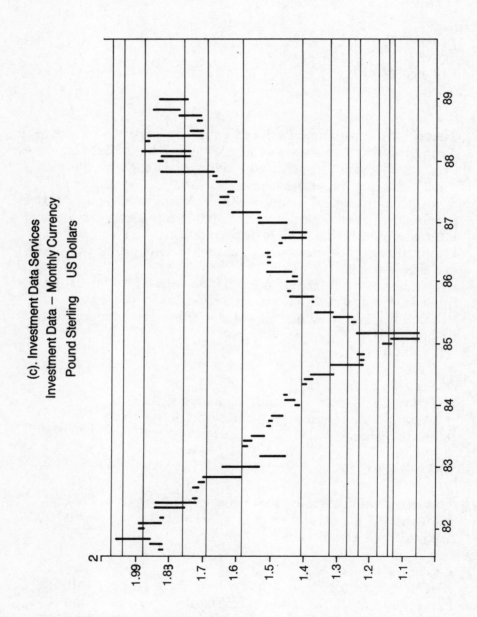

Chart 1   Sterling/US dollar monthly values, March 1981–June 1988

50

corporations in the USA. This is a comfort, but in the US particularly, both the Federal Deposit Insurance Corporation (FDIC) and its sister Federal Savings and Loans Insurance Corporation (FSLIC) rely on subscribers' funds which could prove inadequate in the event of major failures. Both the FDIC and FSLIC have federal backing but deposits could be frozen if Congress delayed making funds available.

In Britain, the clearing banks are closely regulated by the Bank of England and must be regarded as being sound. However, deposits are not insured and delays in withdrawing cash would be possible should a bank or building society encounter liquidity problems.

In both countries, a major failure could trigger a rush to withdraw deposits and there might be a 'bank holiday' similar to that faced by President Roosevelt when he took office in March 1933.

Currency Exchange Losses
If a US depositor had kept funds in Britain from 1981 to 1985 they would have lost over 50 per cent of value; conversely, if a British company had entered into a long-term contract in the US in 1985, the average loss of revenue over three years would be nearly 70 per cent in sterling terms (see Chart 1).

International Default
The level of international debt in the late eighties is now greater than in the late twenties. There are also growing signs of political pressure on governments in the Third World either to freeze or repudiate loan service. These are not new problems. In 1933 Mexico refused to service its external debt and in 1937 Brazil unilaterally suspended debt-service payments. If these and other Latin American countries were to default today, it would wipe out the capital of some of the largest banks in the US and seriously damage two in Britain.

Security of Deposits

In the event of financial crisis at the end of a business cycle there will be a rush to liquidity which will affect all but the most secure institutions. The following instruments will provide security in descending order:

- Treasury Bills issued by governments represent the most secure short-term method of protecting cash. Despite the pressure on governments during a financial crisis, the short-term bill will be honoured.
- Insured bank deposits in the USA are also backed by the Federal Government. However, there might be delays in repayment if the FDIC or FSLIC became insolvent and required Congressional funding consent.
- Short-dated government paper, if redeemable within months, will also be secure but if sold before maturity may suffer some loss of value.
- Unsecured bank deposits of major UK clearing banks will provide security although there may be the possibility of a 'holiday' if the bank is exposed to major Third World debt default.
- Unsecured deposits with institutions will be affected by major changes in their asset value. For example 'thrifts', building societies or secondary banks.

Protection Against Currency Exchange Risks

Cash is required for trading and must be available at the right time for settling debts. The main risk is in exchange rate fluctuations illustrated in Chart 1 and in 'Example of Hedging Currency Risks, p143; for example, if a British company expected a dividend income in US$ from January 1985 to January 1988, the average loss of value in sterling terms would have been nearly one-third.

There are three main methods of protecting cash flow:

- Deposits in several currencies would balance the exchange risks for an international company trading with many nations.
- Forward exchange transactions are a method of buying the appropriate currency in advance for delivery when payment is due.
- Hedging debts or payments is a method of protection

where a value may be 'hedged', through buying (or selling) a futures or option contract that guards against adverse changes in exchange rates.

Introduction to Financial Futures and Options
Reprinted from an Introduction to LIFFE

What are Financial Futures?
A financial futures contract is an agreement to buy or sell, on an organised exchange, a standard quantity of a specific financial instrument or foreign currency at a future date and at a price agreed between two parties. Although contracts are traded between buyer and seller on an exchange floor, each has an obligation not to the other, but to a clearing house. This ensures that the futures market is free from credit risk to a considerable extent.

Standard Quantity
Each contract specifies that it is for a standard quantity, eg $1m.

Specific Financial Instrument
The contract specifies both the type of financial instrument and its 'quality' in terms of such things as coupon rate and maturity.

Delivery Dates
The instruments specified by the contract must be exchanged at or during a specified month in the future, usually in a cycle of March, June, September and December.

Clearing House
LIFFE's clearing house clears and guarantees the Exchange's transactions. Because LIFFE contracts are standardised, with buyers and sellers knowing exactly what they are trading, dealing is convenient and liquid.

Options on Cash and Futures
Traded options are standardised options which grant the buyer the right (but not the obligation) to buy or sell financial

instruments at standard prices and times in the future. Trading is carried out on the exchange floor with the contracts guaranteed by a clearing house. Unlike futures contracts the buyer of options contracts has his risk limited to what he has paid for the option, the option premium. For each expiry date there will be a number of exercise prices for both options to buy and to sell. LIFFE's options contracts have expiry dates in a cycle of March, June, September and December with additional nearby months in a 1–2–3 month cycle for the currency options.

'Calls' and 'Puts'
The buyer of an option has the right, but not the obligation, to buy or sell at a specified future price and can exercise his option at any time before the expiry date. An option to buy is known as a 'call' and an option to sell a 'put'.

'American' or 'European' Options
LIFFE's options are American options as they can be both bought, sold and exercised before expiry. European options on the other hand may not be exercised before expiry.

In-the-money and Out-of-the-money Options
In the case of calls, options with exercise prices *below* the current underlying instruments price are in-the-money and *above* are out-of-the-money. With puts, options with prices *above* the current cash price are in-the-money and *below* are out-of-the-money.

Hedging Techniques

Hedging is used to reduce the risk of loss through adverse price movements in interest rates, currency rates or share prices by taking a position that is equal and opposite to an existing or anticipated position in the cash market. It is impossible to list every potential use of financial futures, but the following two examples show how they can be used to hedge interest rate risks. Appendix 4 shows two examples of currency and interest rate hedging working in practice.

RETAINING THE VALUE OF CASH

To Lock in a Lending Rate

A fund manager may know that he will receive cash for investment in gilts maturing in more than fifteen years in three months' time. Rather than waiting to see what the interest rate will be at that time, he can lock in today's rate by buying Long Gilt futures contracts for delivery in three months' time. If gilt yields then decline, the investor will have to pay a higher price, but the price of the Long Gilt futures contracts will have risen and the fund manager's profits on his futures contract will reduce the effective cost of buying the stock and preserve the return on his funds.

The use of futures locks the fund manager into current rates and if they move contrary to his expectation, there will be a loss on the futures contract offsetting the corresponding gain in the cash market. Forgone cash market profits, if rates fall, are the price of insulation from volatility in interest rates.

To Lock in a Borrowing Rate

A company with a need to borrow in six months' time, which considered that interest rates might rise, would sell financial futures contracts for that date. If rates did rise, the profit from being short of futures would roughly equal the additional borrowing costs.

7
Protecting Receivables

Potential Threat to Cash Flow in Time of Adversity

Receivables comprise about 40 per cent of the net worth of many trading companies and represent the major source of cash flow into a business. At the end of a business cycle there is a danger that the supply of credit dries up and incoming funds will at best slow down and at worst be uncollectable.

The threat is real. Surprisingly, less than 10 per cent of receivables in the UK are protected by some form of underwriting or insurance. There is the additional danger that an increased risk of failure could affect suppliers' ability to maintain deliveries.

This chapter explains how to guard against the potential loss of net worth. Debt insurance and factoring are undoubtedly the most reliable ways of protecting the major portion of the expected cash flow against failure; these methods are described under the first three subheadings of the chapter. Credit risk through bad debt provisions using external sources of analysis do not protect cash flow although they take some recognition of potential failure.

Protection Through Insurance

The flow of income from receivables may be insured in Britain up to a high proportion of their value through one of several brokers, the largest of these being Trade Indemnity plc (TI) protecting over £30bn of sales in 1988. TI is jointly owned by major British and Swiss insurance companies who reinsure most of the risk carried by the company. TI also operates in Australia and provides protection for credit trading through various instruments worldwide.

The Working of Credit Insurance

TI will repay up to 80 per cent of a debt's value in the event of insolvency; the cover may also include work-in-progress in certain trades and industries. Insurance premiums are based on gross sales value and there may be additional fees for debt collection or special services.

TI will work closely alongside credit-control departments which are provided with a set of limits for the major trading accounts – any variations being made by prior agreement. When new accounts are opened, lines of credit below £10,000 are allowed without reference to TI while still receiving credit cover.

Risk Assessment

TI maintains one of the most comprehensive assessments of corporate risk in Britain, placing particular emphasis on the 25 per cent least solvent trading companies. In the UK, 20,000 firms constitute 80 per cent of risk and, of these, 2,000 receive particular attention to ensure that they do not exceed the reinsurance quotas.

Protection Through Debt Factoring

Factoring differs from credit insurance in that in most cases the factor buys an invoice when issued and pays up to 80 per cent of its value within a few days; the balance is paid on maturity. The arrangement is eminently sound and sensible but factoring only represents 25 per cent of insured debts (their presence being resented by many customers). Factors are tough debt collectors.

British factors offer a strong support service to their clients. Most are owned, or have strong links, with clearing banks and have access to the payment record of tens of thousands of customers.

The range of service offered by factors is considerable and, in general, hinges around the quality of protection. Debts protected against default are known as non-recourse factoring; if borne by the vendor, it is recourse factoring. This chapter can only describe the subject in outline and for a more complete treatment, the reader should consult *Factoring and the Accountant in Practice* by F.R. Salinger (see 'Further Reading').

Non-recourse Factoring

Non-recourse factoring implies that the factor takes responsibility for all debts and cannot seek compensation from the vendor in the case of failure. In what is known in the USA as full-line factoring, the factor effectively buys the debts from the seller and takes responsibility for the sales ledger and credit-control function. In this way the factor is responsible for debt collection and the client receives the purchase price (being the face value of the invoice) less charges and a discount for early payment. One variant is maturity factoring where there is no prepayment of debts, which are paid, less charges, on maturity. The debts, however, are protected against non-payment by the customer.

Recourse Factoring

Recourse factoring implies that the ultimate responsibility for debt collection remains with the seller. In the event of default, the factor can claim back pre-payments of bad debts. A further variation of recourse factoring is invoice discounting or confidential factoring, whereby the vendor retains control of the sales ledger and the factor provides interim finance through discounting the invoices.

Comparison Between Credit Insurance and Factoring

Credit insurance is a prudent and relatively cheap method of ensuring that up to 80 per cent of all debts (and some contracts are work-in-progress) will eventually be received. The vendor retains full control of the business and, in addition, receives strong support from a company such as TI.

Non-recourse factoring is an excellent method of both reducing the fixed costs of a business and receiving funds from another source of finance. It is particularly valuable for a small business starting up, where debt security may be more important than margins; there may also be difficulties in raising bank loans on a small asset or revenue base. Misuse of factoring occurs when, with other sources of non-capital finance, it is used to its limit.

Protection Through Bad Debt Provision

As an alternative to credit assurance or factoring, the majority of businesses prefer to protect their debts by measuring their customer's payment risk and then restricting credit if they are unlikely to be paid in full. Potential losses from bad or doubtful debts are then worked out and a provision is made in the accounts for the current year based mainly on historical performance.

This approach relies on the assumption that external events, such as the end of the business cycle, do not change credit worthiness. From reading Chapter 2 – it clearly does.

For example, consider the position of a highly geared distributor that was able to maintain regular payments during the Inflationary Phase of the closing stages of the business cycle – see Chapter 2. The position could change rapidly when interest rates start to rise and consumer spending falls. What was an acceptable balance sheet on a historic basis could now become a disaster and there is almost no way of measuring the outcome from risk analysis methods.

To guard against both company and business cycle risks, the credit controller will need three inputs:–

- A sound means of risk assessment which implies one of the tried methods (or their variants) of measuring corporate solvency described in Appendix 5. The interested reader will find how three different techniques addressed one particular failure.
- An assessment of the stage in the business cycle and the likely risks inherent at any one time. Clearly the most dangerous times are during the early parts of the recession and when it is just over – see Chapters 2, 16 and Appendix 1.
- Judging whether the customer is taking management action appropriate for the stage of the business cycle is described in Chapter 16. Even if a financial crisis will put at risk a number of companies, a board that has taken

sensible counter measures will still prove a sound business partner and the shrewd credit controller will gain good marks from the sales director for keeping open – or even extending – lines of credit.

8

Protecting Inventory

The average level of a trading company's inventory in Britain is around 30 per cent of net worth, about equal to trade creditors. The value of this stockholding will be vulnerable, in the event of a financial crisis, from two directions, obsolescence and excess value for the new level of sales.

Inventory obsolescence will be the result of intense competition from other companies all attempting to maintain their level of sales in a shrinking market sector. One component of this will be a squeeze on margins, another will be an increased rate of product development that will speed up inventory obsolescence.

Reduced sales will make present inventory levels excessive and it will be difficult to reach a new balance without selling a number of items below the purchase price. The cash inflow from the 'fire sale' will be below that needed to pay creditors and additional funds will be needed.

Avoiding Inventory Reduction During a Recession

Considerable advances have been made recently by Materials Requirement Planning (MRP) techniques which have reduced inventory levels by up to 30 per cent. This target has been eclipsed by Japanese companies who need inventory levels of only a few hours using 'Just In Time' (JIT) concepts of management. JIT also fulfils the precise solution to the obsolescence and slow-moving inventory problems posed above.

JIT has its origins in the post-World War II period when younger Japanese managements were given the opportunity to build a new peacetime industrial structure. They took Western (mainly American) techniques of management and adapted these to Japanese traditions of loyalty to the organisation and discipline. Unlike many Western counterparts,

61

these new ideas were pioneered by senior Japanese managements as a competitive tool to gain market share. JIT was not just a handy technique for the production director; it was part of the corporate credo to which top management was totally committed.

The purpose of this chapter is to introduce the concept of JIT without attempting to cover the subject in any sort of detail. It is also a management style that will almost certainly become widely accepted during the nineties.

What is JIT? The following description is by Gavin Bridges of Arthur Young Management Consultants.

Just In Time (JIT) Fits the Requirement

The River of Inventory
Traditionally inventory has been held to hide problems. For example, buffer stocks are held because of the possibility of scrapping a batch or because of late deliveries from suppliers. High inventories are held due to large batches being loaded to the shops because of long machine set-up times.

The philosophy of JIT reverses this traditional thinking. Rather than holding high inventory to hide or smother problems, the JIT philosophy is to lower the level of inventory to expose problems. The philosophy is analogous to a river of inventory where the level of the river represents the level of inventory and the rocks on the river bed represent problems.

The JIT philosophy is to lower the level of the river to expose *the* major company problem. In Fig 9 this is represented by the 'Inaccurate Stock Records' rock. The management task now is to set up a team (usually multi-disciplined) to solve that problem using some of the many JIT techniques available. Top management commitment is needed to live with the problem until the team has succeeded. The natural tendency to raise the level of inventory temporarily to get round or hide the problem must be avoided. If you do this you are paying twice: firstly for the increase in inventory and secondly for the inefficiencies caused by the problem. Additionally, if the pressure is not there, there is less chance of the problem being solved. It is therefore of paramount importance for top management to understand and be committed to grasping the nettle firmly.

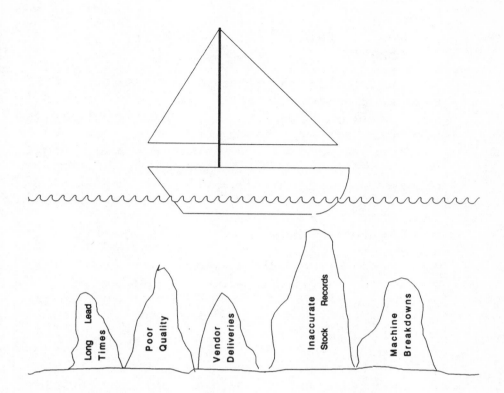

Fig. 9   The River of Inventory (*Gavin Bridges of Arthur Young Management Consultants*)

Introduction to JIT

Work

JIT has the goal of reducing inventory to near zero levels. It aims to achieve this by making production immediately responsive to demand. For example, Nissan carries ten hours of work-in-progress compared to an average of fifteen days for an equivalent British company. Production is 'pulled' through the factory by demand, thus there is no inventory awaiting further processing. In practice sub-contractors of many Japanese companies are given ten days' notice for component delivery at a specified time. Pulling is not an easy option. It requires a high degree of machine and tooling maintenance, readiness at each stage of the process and high quality levels. The traditional Western policy is to budget levels of sales and to make sure that the process operates to push work through factories to allow for inefficiencies.

Analysis

JIT is achieved through rigorous analysis into every cause of inefficiency; these are divided between chronic (re-occuring) and random problems. Chronic problems are defined as being ever present, for example, a 'normal' high level of inventory, a regular machine breakdown or a tool change that occupies a shift. A JIT-based company will form a multi-disciplinary team to investigate and solve the problem as part of a continual drive for challenging previously accepted norms.

JIT analytic techniques have three stages: symptom, cause and remedy. The aim is to brainstorm all the possible reasons for a problem before identifying and rectifying the real cause. JIT adopts the Ishikawa or 'fishbone' method of classifying causes in their origins of manpower, machines, method or materials.

Design

JIT starts with designers who need to take into account the complete process from raw material through to customer satisfaction. It is estimated that 80 per cent of all failures of quality, tooling, material and methods can be attributable to faults at the design stage. There is also the problem of inventory write-off if components become obsolete due to design changes or modifications.

Supply Chain

JIT requires new management of the supply chain in which relationships incorporate mutual trust and dependency compared to the Western policy of multi-sourcing. Under a JIT system the customer will establish a long-term harmonisation of standards to ensure that supplies (of the correct quality and specification) will be available at the precise time needed for production.

Quality

Quality is integral to production and reject rates of parts per million (PPM) are expected targets compared to the 5–10 per cent tolerated in the West. Quality starts with design and works through at each stage: as a rule of thumb it is reckoned that a mistake rectified at the design stage costs £1, in the factory £10 and in the field, £100. In a JIT factory, operators check their own work and any falling below the quality standard is a cause not for criticism but for rectification.

JIT is integral with Company Quality Improvement (CQI), the Japanese approach to aligning all levels of the company to the belief that theirs is the best business and they are the best performers. This belief starts at the highest level and work is carried out by multi-disciplinary cells involving everyone. Quality circles are just part of employee involvement.

Group Approach to JIT
Getting started with JIT depends upon the organisation. If there is one particular source of inefficiency this should be tackled first by a select group of specialists in order to demonstrate the effectiveness of the concept. Where there is no one dominant issue, a deliberate reduction in the level of inventory by say 10 per cent will expose the problem and have the desired effect.

9

Managing Investments

Investments become highly volatile towards the end of an economic cycle when excess liquidity has to find an outlet. In the final stages, cash moves either into physical assets (commodities) as happened during 1980 or into financial assets (stock market) as in 1929 and 1987. In either case, there is a massive rise before a precipitous crash. Any investment strategy will need to take account of each phase and change with it.

This chapter is written for those who wish to work out an investment strategy – for example, with their pension fund or private portfolio managers. The proposed investment programme is based on historical research; readers should come to their own conclusions before making investment decisions.

There are four sections:

- Strategy during phase 1 – inflation.
- Strategy during phase 2 – crisis.
- Strategy during phase 3 – decline.
- An approach to chart analysis.

Strategy During Phase 1 – Inflation

An inflationary period is a dangerous time to be holding equities because of conflicting signals. Certainly, business is good and profits are rising but so is the credit that fuels demand. Historically there has always come a moment when concern for the future overrides the present and there is a scramble for liquidity.

These are some of the leading indicators:

- Commodity prices increase during an inflationary period and will show either in the rise of individual materials or by collective indices. The two main indicators are the Commodity Research Bureau (CRB) Futures Index and the Reuters Commodity Index. Both are produced daily and vary somewhat in their constituents. The CRB is more heavily weighted towards soft commodities while Reuters has a greater bias towards metals.

- Inflationary expectations rise as a nation's economy comes up against capacity restraints. Each country has its own indicators: there is the Consumer Price Index (CPI) in the USA and the Retail Price Index (RPI) in Britain.
- Interest rates rise when the authorities attempt to damp down excess credit in the economy, an event that has happened four times in the USA since World War II (see Appendix 1).

Investment Strategy

During this period consider a portfolio comprising a high proportion of short-dated government issues that will provide income without sacrificing capital value. Also consider investing a quarter in stocks and physical assets that will increase in value during inflation; the balance should be in cash. A sensible disposition might include:

Cash on deposit	15 per cent
Short-dated government stocks including German, Swiss and US issues depending upon currency trends; also index-linked stocks	60 per cent
Gold, silver or platinum bullion, coins and related stock	25 per cent.

Strategy During Phase 2 – Crisis

Before the peak of the crisis the stock market is most likely to have reversed, as interest rates continue to rise and the yield curve becomes negative (ie the yield on US Treasury Bills exceeds those of the Treasury Bond - see Appendix 1). At the peak, consider switching the bulk of the portfolio into long-dated government bonds.

Watch for these indicators:

- Commodities peak, keep a check on the CRB or Reuters Index.
- Treasury Bond and Treasury Bill yields peak.
- Real estate values fall when the yield curve goes negative.

Consider the following portfolio disposition:

Cash on deposit	5 per cent
Long-dated bonds and governments stocks	85 per cent
Gold bullion or coins	10 per cent

Strategy During Phase 3 – Decline

Typically, bear markets last from a third to half the length of the preceding bull market and there are likely to be a number of steep declines with intervening rallies.

The best-known bear market was in the early thirties described in more detail in 'An Approach to Understanding Chart Analysis' opposite. It is possible to make considerable profits trading bear markets, using options and other financial instruments but these are an individual choice and are not described in this section.

The rate of change for various markets has varied in the past with interest rates and commodities the most volatile. Watch for the following:

- Commodities start a rapid fall, watch the indices and individual materials.
- Bond and Bill yields fall rapidly but watch for a secondary rally some months later, a feature of every bear market.

The portfolio proposed below differs little from Phase 2 except that there has been a partial move out of government long-dated stocks into commercial debentures and stock. Gold is retained for the secondary interest rates 'spike'. Be prepared for a rally in the stock market after the end of the bear market.

Long-dated government stock including
   foreign issues   75 per cent
Debentures and convertible loan stocks   15 per cent
Gold bullion and coins   10 per cent

An Approach to Understanding Chart Analysis

Technical analysis is a method of reading charts of prices or indices in order to predict future movements. Reading charts has fascinated mankind for many years and a number of systems have been devised.

Traditional analysis is concerned with prices or indices that move in trend channels and find support or resistance depending upon past patterns. Other techniques involve the use of moving averages, time cycles, volumes and relative movements that are used in computer trading systems. This is an extensive subject and many books have been written about it.

In addition to traditional analysis there are two main technical systems devised by W.D. Gann and R.N. Elliott respectively.

Gann was a student of geometry and natural numbers, which enabled him to predict (and benefit from) the Wall Street Crash of 1929. Elliott, by contrast, was wiped out in 1929 but subsequently devised a system working on natural rhythms that defined the movement of markets; he also made use of a number series defined by Fibonacci, an Italian mathematician. The two systems are described briefly and the interested reader should consult the 'Further Reading' list.

Chart 2 is of the Dow Jones Industrial Averages from mid-1928 to 1933 which will be used to illustrate both systems. W.D. Gann believed that the likely future movement of prices or indices might be judged through drawing lines from significant points on the chart. For example, in Chart 2:

1   Diagonal fan lines may be drawn from high and low points which contain future price movements. Taking the low of June 1928, the lines defining the prices until September 1929 rose at the rate of two points per week and four points per week respectively. The break of the 2 by 1 line

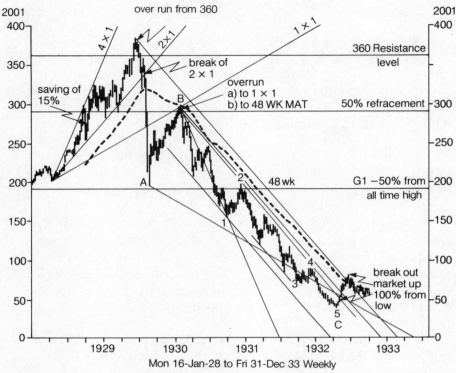

Chart 2   Dow Jones Industrial Averages (1928–33).

was the end of that stage of the bull market; furthermore, when the down line from point B was broken in July 1932 it was the end of the long bear market.

2   The second group of lines are horizontal and refer to 50 per cent movements from previous high and low points. For example, 50 per cent from the all-time high of 3 September 1929 is at point A, the precise point where the market turned in November. The rally to point B was just over the 50 per cent retracement and from point B through to C the rallies often retraced 50 per cent of the previous fall.

3   Gann analysts would have been further warned that the market was in potential decline by the break (and return) through the resistance level of 360 (Gann used the division of the 360° circle for timing and price levels, 360 being the most significant).

R.N. Elliott's basic diagram is shown in Chart 3 and through reference to the previous chart of the Dow Jones.

1   The classical Elliott curve is made of five upwaves followed by three down. Waves 1, 3 and 5 are impulse while 2 and 4 are corrective. On the downside, waves A and C are impulse while B is corrective. Referring to the 1929 chart, the A, B and C waves wave are clearly shown, with wave C being made up of a number of smaller impulse and corrective waves.

2   After defining the major movements, Elliott measures the extent of the impulses and corrections through the Fibonacci ratio 0.618. This is particularly useful when judging the timing and amplitude of the impulse and corrective waves.

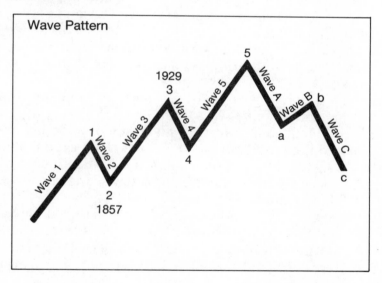

Chart 3   Classic Elliot Wave Pattern

Reprinted from *Elliott Wave Prinicple*

10
Financing Fixed Assets

Fixed assets represent around 60 per cent of the net worth of Hoare Govett's Quoted UK plc model. It has been the custom for property and plant to be funded through equity and term loans but within the last five years alternative methods of financing have been growing. This chapter is particularly concerned with the financing of plant, while Appendix 3 considers more flexible arrangements for negotiating property leases.

Leasing plant and equipment has become popular since SSAP 21 made leasing payments (except for cars) allowable for corporation tax. All types of plant can be leased and in 1987 the major demand was for computer and office equipment. Conversely, existing plant may be sold to lessors as part of a sale and leaseback agreement.

Extended credit is used by business to fund primarily motor cars and other vehicles but ranging through property, farm equipment and industrial plant. Unlike leasing, title may pass to the purchaser who can then claim capital allowances against taxation. Credit financing is widely used as a sales aid to consumers, the vendor often acting as an agent for the finance house.

Both leasing and credit contracts are handled through members of the Finance Houses Association (FHA) and the Equipment Leasing Association (ELA). The headquarters of both the FHA and the ELA have contributed data for this chapter. The chapter has two sections:

- Use of assets through leasing.
- Instalment credit.

Use of Assets Through Leasing

Leasing is a method of providing the benefits of an asset

while ownership lies with the lessor. The lessee has the use of equipment for the period of agreement during which time it is hoped that the cash flow will more than cover the charges and interest; the longer-term finance leases are usually calculated from a variable rate of interest.

Leasing has the clear advantage over outright purchase because payment is made during the period of cash generation. The owner benefits from a regular cash stream and capital allowances. Over one-third of leasing contracts are for finance leasing which assumes a write-off over five years. Operating leases assume that the asset will have a residual value and is saleable after the lease expires. The different terms used to describe leasing arrangements are:

- Finance leasing is the term given to long-term contracts when the asset is leased over a five-year period and is deemed to have no residual value. Except for cars, the leasing charges are fully allowable against corporation tax although the tax treatment requires the asset to be shown in the balance sheet with an associated charge. The terms of a finance lease can be negotiated flexibly to meet the cash flow anticipated by the lessee. At the end of the term, the asset is written-off by the lessor and the lease may be continued at a peppercorn rate.
- Operating leases are generally for shorter periods than a finance lease and cover items such as cars, computers, or trucks which retain a value at the end of the contract. The tax treatment is the same as for a finance lease except that no record of the lease needs to appear in the balance sheet. Shorter-term leases are normally negotiated at fixed rates of interest.
- Contract hire is a special form of operating lease where the lessor takes full responsibility for providing operational machinery and sometimes the driver. It is particularly used for the hire of items such as fork-lift trucks, commercial vehicles, compressors and other items of static or mobile plant.
- Rental, hiring and plant-hire are all forms of short-term leasing, for example a construction or repair contract. The lessor will keep items such as excavators, trucks, vans

etc in stock and will provide a full insurance, maintenance and replacement service.

Instalment Credit

Instalment credit is primarily used for consumer purchase. Finance houses will advance cash for the purchase of an asset which is repaid over the life of a contract with associated interest and other charges. In a credit contract, ownership of the asset may pass to the purchaser and in this case some other security will be required as collateral until repayment is completed.

As with leasing, long-term contracts are negotiated at floating rates determined by the lender at a set margin above a widely advertised level, such as the Finance Houses Base Rate. Shorter-term deals tend to be at a fixed rate of interest that cannot be varied over the life of the contract. There are a number of forms of instalment credit:

- Hire-purchase is a common form of instalment credit where title passes progressively to the buyer over the life of the contract. The buyer may claim the capital allowances against taxation irrespective of any delay in passing the title.
- Conditional sale is a variation of instalment credit where title only passes after the last payment.
- Credit sale is where ownership passes at the time of purchase, the payments being made over the contract period. Where required, the credit house will need alternative security as collateral.
- Personal and commercial loans are available from finance houses, repayable with interest and charges during the contract. The rate of interest is fixed and collateral will be required.

11
Raising Funds During a Recovery

The bankers and shareholders closest to a business will be relieved when a new manager is appointed to launch the rescue operation. Both parties will have been in despair that nothing was being done and now will be supportive of plans to save their loan or investment.

Relationships during the first few months are important. Bankers have a confidential relationship with their customers but great care will be needed with shareholders to avoid any possibility of insider dealing. One approach may be the appointment of a committee of shareholders who have agreed not to deal while they are privy to confidential information.

Once an action plan has been worked out (following the programme in Chapter 3), the next step is to raise a bridging loan to finance the recovery. Almost always, this will come from banks because they have security which the shareholders do not possess; risk capital is difficult to raise until a company is in a position to resume dividend payments. Timing is important. It is much easier to raise funds when an economic recovery is under way than after a recession; this affects assumptions made in the cash forecast and the sustainable level of debt.

The first step is to complete the recovery programme and demonstrate that there is a positive cash flow. Next it should be possible to increase borrowings to invest in the continuing businesses. Finally, shareholders can be approached for funds to continue growth and reduce debt. These three stages are described in more detail:

RAISING FUNDS DURING A RECOVERY

Stage 1   Returning to a Positive Cash Flow

A company's banker will be delighted to see any plans for turning assets into cash provided that the money is applied to reducing debt. Being prudent, prior permission will have been sought to sell assets over which there is a charge. A successful recovery programme is likely to be marked by a reduction in net worth and the banker may wish to protect his position by reducing borrowing limits. This should be resisted. A recovery programme needs cash to buy off liabilities and there will be a time-lag before this can be funded by asset sales. Of first importance is that debt and cost are reduced and profits revived. Negotiations will be simplified if the presentation includes the following:

- A summary of financial performance over five years with a commentary on significant events.
- An analysis of the present position which could conveniently take the form of Figs. 1 and 2, an analysis of costs and assets (described in Chapter 3).
- A summary of the disposal programme ('sells') with costs, time-scales and realisable values.
- Cash-flow forecast of the retained activity ('holds'), an estimated level of continuing profitability and the bridging loans needed for the recovery implementation.
- Summary of the management structure showing the changes that have been made at board and senior management level, also plans for recruitment and new responsibilities.

Stage 2   Increasing the Loan Facility

As recovery proceeds, it will be possible to show the 'holds' and 'sells' separately in the monthly accounts and a copy should be circulated to the bank(s). In due course, the 'sells' will disappear and the cash flow will become positive. This is an excellent time to request an increased loan facility for boosting the performance of the 'holds'. The bank manager will be expecting this approach and this will be an opportunity to negotiate an increase in the facility for at least next year's trading.

RAISING FUNDS DURING A RECOVERY

Stage 3   Going to the Market

If the company is quoted, recovery action will be quickly spotted by analysts who continually comb the market for new 'situations'. One possible response could be a take-over offer, a potential bidder perceiving that assets could be picked up quite cheaply. Fighting a bid at this stage is not easy because shareholders may be tempted to clear their books of what had been previously an embarrassment. The chances of a successful defence will be improved if institutional shareholders have been kept in touch with progress.

If still independent, the task is to raise sufficient funds for at least three years ahead. Any less time tends to aggravate shareholders, called upon repeatedly for cash. Fund raising is outside the scope of this book but, whatever the source, extensive information will be needed for a prospectus that will be tested by the company's auditor and financial adviser. This should include the following:

- Summary of financial performance over five years with a commentary on the important events.
- Summary of the action plan and the results to date showing the improvement in margins and debt levels.
- An assessment of present markets and a penetration target for existing and intended products.
- A sales forecast for the next – say – three years and the likely margins and dividends payable. The third year should be accompanied by a pro-forma balance sheet.
- An evaluation of major assets such as property.
- A summary of the senior management, their positions and shareholdings.

PART THREE

FIXED COST
REDUCTION

*Three new techniques of reducing costs
without harming present business*

12

Third Generation Fixed Cost Reduction

The first eleven chapters of this book have been concerned with proven methods of corporate recovery through funding debt and reducing costs. If these remedies are administered in time an ailing business will be restored to financial health.

A discerning management will realise that this is only the first step along a continuous process of cost reduction described in this chapter as Third Generation techniques because they follow previous cost-cutting methods.[1]

Each of these new methods is completely in line with *The Third Wave*, a remarkably prescient book written by Alvin Toffler and published in 1980. Toffler believes that the concentration of the industrial revolution will give way to more individual forms of working which may be carried out remotely from the office or factory. In one sense, this is a return to the conditions before the nineteenth century when many people conducted their trade from home.

Third Generation Ideas

Third generation concepts reduce costs by creating new independent units which tackle both operational and staff

---

[1]First generation methods were widely practised in the sixties and seventies following mergers. Two (or more) not dissimilar companies were amalgamated in the hope that one set of overheads would serve both, and the 'released' assets were sold for deployment elsewhere.

The second generation of overhead reduction was more subtle and took place in the early eighties. City-based companies transferred staff away from expensive accommodation into country towns within easy reach of London. Staffing levels were also reduced through new technology and sub-contracting services. Other companies reduced their head office expenses, replacing them more cheaply at subsidiary level.

functions. Agency working and franchising devolve the responsibility for promotion, service, distribution, etc away from main-line management to independently financed units, who act as agents or licensees. Remote working, however, is mainly concerned with staff who, after becoming independent, sub-contract their services for a fee. The methods are described in detail in Chapters 13, 14 and 15. To summarise:

- Franchising (Chapter 13) is a fast-growing technique for expanding retail distribution and services. It can also be used for reducing the fixed cost of existing branches and depots. The singular advantage of franchising is that independent individuals or companies buy the assets and facilities and operate these under licence from the parent. The new owners are then responsible for all aspects of administration, accounting, sales and operations.
- Remote working (Chapter 14) is a technique pioneered within the Rank Xerox organisation for reducing costs during a major reconstruction in the early eighties. The plan makes employees, serving at many levels of a company, independent while still working at least part of the time for the parent.
- Agency working (Chapter 15) is a technique developed in the USA replacing the fixed expense of a sales or service network with independent individuals or companies working on commission. The plan could include a buy-out of the sales organisation by employees as part of a new relationship with the parent. The contract gives some mutual exclusivity while allowing the sales force freedom to represent other non-competing products. Agency working can cover other outside staff such as service personnel, telephone salespeople and merchandisers. Where the agent takes the name of the parent it may be a franchise.

Third Generation Management Styles

Third generation ideas are concerned with converting authority to flexibility. What was under direct control is now dispersed to independently financed units tied contractually to the original parent. Some of the facets of the new style are:

- Policy making will be concerned less with structure and more with flexibility. Less with market share and more with balance sheet strength. Less with reducing direct costs and more with reducing fixed costs. The changing emphasis moves from the perception of making money through inflation to commanding sales during disinflation, from employing people to contracting their services.
- New management skills will be needed by the company (or core) manager and independent worker alike. A core manager will need to replace directing with contracting skills in order to define, price, contract and monitor individuals supplying a service or performing a task.
- New personal skills will be needed by individuals to promote, administer, finance and control, whether they operate under the umbrella of a franchise or as an agency or remote worker.
- Introducing independent working should only be undertaken when there has been a thorough study and agreement that both parent company and the individual will benefit from the proposal. Once a plan has been agreed, it is important that it is fully tested by selected individuals over a period of six to twelve months.

Introducing the Third Generation

No plan can be successful without offering both parties a profitable future, so any programme has two essential components. Firstly, confidence gained by testing the plan and secondly, top-level support within the company. The three stages involve making a feasibility study, planning the programme and proving the pilot scheme over a period:

- A feasibility study should be undertaken by the 'change driver' appointed and supported by the parent board. He or she should work with a small team aided by an outside specialist. The aim is to work out the opportunity for reducing fixed costs by any one of the three methods, singly or in combination. This can succeed only if the newly independent unit can foresee a profitable future. The study should be confidential.

- The planning stage is only possible if the feasibility study is positive. The most important component is to detail the heads of agreement between the two sides before the contract becomes a legal document. Other matters flow from the agreement. These include manuals describing procedures, promotion and other material, training, individual testing and the introduction of pilot schemes.
- The pilot schemes test the agreed plan over a period of six to twelve months. The first pilot unit should only involve a very few people so that any mistakes may be remedied within a short time. If there are to be failures, these would be limited. At the end of the period, people at many levels should be involved to work out the best balance and to evaluate the next stage. After a successful second pilot test, the programme may be implemented with a high level of confidence.

Third Generation in Historical Context

An analysis of the economic cycles described in Appendix 1 suggests that there are considerable parallels between the history of the United States during the twenties and the eighties. The parallels would seem to be strengthened by the election of Mr George Bush as Republican President in 1988; the last time that three Republicans were elected consecutively was when Hoover followed Coolidge in 1928 and both men faced a democratic congress. In addition, present debt levels are similar to, or greater than, those of sixty years ago and there are other similarities. This is not to argue that history will repeat itself, it is sufficient that it provokes an interest in this period.

The events of the twenties and thirties are important as a backdrop for the changes introduced by the Third Generation. The thirties saw the birth of the large company on the assumption that economies of scale would produce greater efficiency; in Britain it was the start of nationalisation when airlines, electricity generation and broadcasting were brought under state control. In the USA, the New Deal introduced the Tennessee Valley Authority (TVA), the Public Works Administration (PWA) and other federal initiatives.

Industry in the UK followed with the successful merging of chemical companies to form ICI and the attempts to merge steel companies by Clarence Hatry. A chronicle of these events is set out in Appendix 6.

In some ways the concentration was necessary because trade in the thirties was conducted by cartels and to be big was an advantage. Economies of scale, however, could only be realised by a large clerical staff specialising in one particular department or function. If a service was needed a department was set up and a specialist brought in as a manager.

The trend towards size continued after World War II with the nationalisation of many industries in Britain and rationalisation of some still in the private sector. The perceived benefits of scale continued but the need for large staff was being eroded by new techniques such as data processing and increasingly productive machines.

Changes Leading to the Nineties

As has been seen, the first steps to reduce the cost of large staffs were quite crude but over the years new patterns or 'generations' started to emerge. The changes implied by the third generation methods are radically altering management styles. Size and power were previously regarded as being the mark of success but they are likely to give way to dispersal and flexibility. In a sense, the concentration of the thirties will become the decentralisation of the nineties.

13
Fixed Cost Reduction Through Franchising

It is impressive how many franchise operations such as MacDonald's, Kentucky Fried Chicken and Tie Rack are forming part of new shopping centres. The franchisors have made this very rapid progress by attracting companies and individuals to put their own money – and that of their backers – into new ventures.

Franchising is also used to reduce costs and generate cash by selling existing branches or depots to present (or new) management. Franchising changes the employer/employee relationship into a contract between independently financed companies, the new owners taking the cost and administrative responsibility previously borne by the parent.

This chapter will examine:

- The franchising idea.
- The choice between owning branches or franchising.
- A case history of unwinding a branch network.
- How to set up a franchise.

(See also Appendices 7–10).

The Franchising Idea

Franchising is a marketing concept. At its heart is a contractual relationship between a parent company (franchisor) and a franchisee. The franchisor possesses a branded product or service which it licenses to an independent person or company, the franchisee. The franchisee is a self-contained business with no capital ties with the parent company; the licence specifies a 'format' within which the franchisee will operate. Agreements cover a wide range of distributive, retail and service operations, from office cleaning programmes costing thousands of pounds to sophisticated computer distribution costing hundreds of thousands.

Two particular methods of franchising demonstrate the extent of the opportunities. One is business format franchising, the other licensing:

- The business format franchise is the most complete method of franchising whereby the franchisor, in exchange for a fee, offers a total business system to the franchisee. The business format franchise assumes, in many cases, that the franchisees have few skills other than the will to succeed and the ability to raise funds for setting themselves up in business.

   The franchisor offers a proven system of business that has been tried and tested in pilot schemes. The format includes a nationally supported and protected brand name, complete operating procedures and a course of training for working as an independent business. When starting, help is given to find premises (if needed), the provision of the necessary tools, sales material and documentation etc. There is also an opportunity for conferences, mutual support from other franchisees, and training both at site and at head office.

   The franchisees are offered a unique experience of working for themselves and owning their own business. They pay an initial fee for business training and a royalty on sales. There is a legal obligation to operate the franchise in accordance with the format and a penalty for failure after a warning – usually through forced sale or buy-back.
- Licensing, unlike franchising, does not imply a proven format; it offers the licensee the opportunity to exploit a business name, system or know-how. There is no franchise fee payable for the whole package although there will be expenses for agreed services. Unlike a franchisee, a licence holder does not necessarily have the right to sell the licence to a third party – unless through prior agreement.

The principles, rights and benefits of franchising are set out in more detail in Appendices 7 and 8.

The Choice Between Owning Branches and Franchising

The cost and capital advantages of franchising are shown in the following example which compares ownership of a typical retail or service branch with the same business if franchised.

Impact on Income
It will be recalled that a parent company's income derives from royalties on sales generated by the franchisee (who is an independently financed businessman); experience shows that the extra motivation often adds some 20 per cent to revenue. A franchisee is a self-contained independent unit responsible for policing its own pilfering, monitoring its own costs and requiring minimum management supervision from the head office.

	Company Owned Branch		Franchised Branch	
	£	%	£	%
Sales	500,000	100		
Gross Margin	225,000	45		
Direct Costs	150,000	30		
Management Fee			37,500	7.5
Head Office Costs	37,500	7.5	25,000	5
Head Office Income	37,500	7.5	12,500	2.5
Head Office Return on Sales		7.5		33.3

Fig. 10   Return of branch income

Fig 14 shows how a branch with sales of £500,000 generates a head office income of £37,500. Should the same business be franchised, the head office would receive a 7.5 per cent royalty (note 7.5 per cent is at the lower end of royalties extending to 15 per cent), from which is deducted the reduced administrative fixed cost of running a franchise. (Note the example ignores any benefits for the parent

88

company by the continuing product supply or increasing franchisee sales, usually 20 per cent.) There is a lower level of income per branch but the lost income can be made up by opening more branches at a marginal capital cost.

Impact on Capital

The example continues with a comparison of the return on capital between a branch and a franchise. Setting up a branch requires an outlay which includes the site, fixtures and fittings, stock and launching expenses. For the franchise there is the expense of franchisee support. The return on capital of the franchise is 125 per cent compared with 35.7 per cent for the branch – see Fig 11.

	Company Owned Branch	Franchised Branch
£	£	
Site premium	30,000	
Fixtures and fittings	20,000	
Stock	50,000	
Training/staff services		10,000
Launch	5,000	
TOTAL	105,000	10,000
Annual profit	37,500	12,500
% Return on Investment	35.7%	125%

Fig. 11   Return on capital employed at branch level

A Case History of Unwinding a Branch Network

Industrial Services Company (ISC) provides a maintenance service to factories and offices where it is competing with both in-house functions and similar facilities provided locally. The latest operating statement and balance sheet are set out in Appendix 9.

Although ISC and its parent company are well known nationally there had been little benefit from the brand name as business was won mainly on price. The company's trading performance showed a return on assets of barely 10 per cent with little advantage to be gained from expansion. The cost of opening up a new branch was around £70,000 which only served to increase the borrowings with a marginal impact on the bottom line. The abbreviated position is as follows:

- Sales for 1987 were £6,700,000 with a pre-tax income of only £60,000. The company employed 290 persons with a ratio of sales per employee of £23,000.
- Assets of £538,000 disguised a loan from the parent company of £1,650,000 which had been needed to fund past losses and open new branches.

An evaluation was made of the business to assess the impact of franchising. These were the results:

- Branding and potential. It was confirmed that the brand name was well established with customers and that there was considerable potential for opening up new branches as the services were required on a local basis.
- Sales. Experience has shown that the added commitment of franchisees increases sales from 20 per cent to 40 per cent; from the same outlets additional branches could be opened at minimum additional cost.
- Negotiations for converting wholly owned branches into separately owned companies needed to include the transfer of pension rights and arrangements for redundancy where employees would be losing their statutory entitlement.
- Organisation. The transfer to franchisees of branch management allowed a deployment within ISC away from administration. Skills are concentrated in development, marketing, opening new franchises, training and support. The saving of at least two layers of management allows a higher quality of staff to be employed within the cost envelope. Overall the output per person has increased over threefold to £73,800.
- Control and support. The franchise format specified in the pilot schemes (and confirmed in the contract) requires a tight control of quality and a high level of commercial support. This enables ISC to support the brand name locally and nationally, and to insist on continuing standards.

- Performance. The return on capital has been increased from around 10 to 54 per cent from the same number of branches. This is a minimum level that could be expected from service franchises.
- The balance sheet which had a gearing of well in excess of 300 per cent now becomes cash rich having paid back all its loans.

How to Set Up a Franchise

This section has been compiled in conjunction with the Centre for Franchise Marketing (CFM).

Franchising a new existing network is not dissimilar to setting up an administration. Each requires a detailed understanding of the operation to be performed, a verification of the calculated benefits and an ability to attract the right people. The subject will be covered in three stages:

- Stage 1   Feasibility study.
- Stage 2   Franchise plan.
- Stage 3   Pilot schemes.

Stage 1   Feasibility Study
This is an examination, usually carried out with the aid of a consultant, to discover the potential for franchising and the benefits that would be offered to both parties. Stage 1 will be illustrated by reference to a feasibility study that was carried out in conjunction with the board of a plant hire company (PHC), (Appendix 10).

There were three parts of the study:

- Positioning in the market-place of the product or service is an important factor for attracting potential franchisees who will be committing their savings. The parent company will be able to supply details of the market and the competition, but this will need to be checked by the consultant who will be viewing the potential through the eyes of the franchisee. An individual working from home can feel very vulnerable if the environment is more harsh than he was led to expect.

91

As will be seen from Appendix 10, PHC has a leading position in the plant hire business in Britain with 22 depots supporting an excellent administrative and technical organisation. The aim is to franchise the field service side of the plant care which supplies independent operators with a similar standard of service to that enjoyed by hire fleet customers. The study showed that the infrastructure was capable of supporting franchisees at little additional cost. Furthermore, the market was available for a number of independent engineers offering a plant care service within a PHC franchise framework.

- Franchisee operations would be directed from the PHC depots but the engineers would be trained and encouraged to make new customer contacts as part of building up their own business. Every feasibility study needs to consider the practical *modus operandi* of a franchise, and to visualise how independent businesses can operate under the parent company umbrella.

- Financial considerations are based on projected income of franchisees and the net revenue to the franchisor once the setting-up costs have been covered. At the feasibility stage it is only possible to estimate the income of an individual franchisee based on the present revenues from employees; this is often less than they realise because independent people become highly motivated and their productivity increases – see experience with ISC above. The financial appraisal will cover the costs of setting up the franchise plan, the pilot schemes (see Stage 3) and the franchise fee paid by the franchisee on signing the agreement.

The report should also show the savings of capital and costs should the whole service be franchised. In the case of PHC, it is estimated in Appendix 10 that each franchise would save vehicle and associated capital of around £20,000 and costs including depreciation of over £22,000. There is an additional unquantified administrative cost of employing extra engineers.

The financial modelling by CFM showed that it should be possible to generate additional head office income of over £400,000 after the third year through the appointment of between sixty-six and seventy-two franchisees.

Stage 2 Franchise Plan

Once the feasibility study has been accepted by the potential franchisor, the next stage is to generate a franchise plan that covers all aspects of the programme until the appointment of the first pilot scheme. There are a number of important components in the franchise plan, the most significant being:

- The appointment of a change driver to mastermind and control the project for the franchisor. He or she should be a highly motivated executive with an excellent knowledge of the business to be franchised. The change driver will be responsible for mobilising the resources of the head office to support the programme.
- The franchise manual and prospectus. The manual should be written under the direction of the change driver to include all the operating procedures that the franchisor requires of the franchisee. This is a comprehensive document. The prospectus sets out the full details of the franchise.
- Promotion material is provided by the franchisor as part of the franchise kit. It will include sales brochures, direct mail letters, advertising support and the appropriate training in telephone selling. The franchise kit will also include stationery and the necessary internal documentation and forms.
- The franchise agreement is an essential part of the contract as it defines the precise entitlements and obligations between the parties.
- Training franchisees in the techniques and procedures defined in the manual is an important introduction for individuals many of whom have never been self-employed. The course lasts for about a week and includes practical working of a franchise as well as the book-keeping procedures within the business and with head office.

Stage 3 Pilot Scheme

It is good practice to start at least three company-owned pilot schemes usually with volunteers from present employees who will test the franchising procedures laid down under the franchise plan. It is important that the schemes are placed in areas that will be representative of the overall plan and they will need to be closely supervised to ensure that all modifications to the written procedures are duly recorded in the master documents. Depending upon the type of franchise, the pilot testing will need at least six to twelve months proving period before more franchisees should be appointed.

14
Fixed Cost Reduction Through Remote Working

This is one of three chapters describing third generation methods of reducing the fixed costs of employing staff. Each is important because they are integral to a more decentralised and flexible method of running a business. They are also important for the individual seeking a more independent working life.

Remote working enables a business to be run at a lower fixed cost than before without losing the skills of key staff. The ideas are simple, well tried and made possible for many by the use of modern communications.

The chapter is divided into three parts. Firstly, an introduction to the subject. Secondly, an explanation of two notable examples of remote working in practice. Thirdly, for the serious reader who wishes to go into the subject in depth.

What is Remote Working?

The fixed expenses of a business are essential for smooth and prudent running. For instance, an accounts team is needed to keep the books and a salesman to deal with customers. In a small business it may be one and the same person, for a large company it will run into several hundreds of people. As a business grows, there is a tendency to recruit specialists such as market researchers, financial planners and other professionals. These people are essential to planning and control but are not operational. If staff are city-based they are also expensive to employ; for every £1 spent in salaries, city-based office professionals cost an additional £2.

Remote working allows a company to reduce the cost of

staff. Some will be able to work for themselves away from the business while still supplying a service; others may still work full-time but be based at home or remotely from the parent.

There are a number of benefits:

- The company is able to reduce more than 50 per cent of the costs of employing staff, including moving into smaller office accommodation. Communication with the remote workers is through some form of linked computers – a network; however, the link is more important for some tasks than others.
- Some professionals are encouraged to work for other non-competing clients while still supplying the original service to the parent company (work is contracted and performed on a fee basis). Others are fully or partly paid depending upon the work and the circumstances.
- Overall productivity has been found to increase by as much as 100 per cent. One major factor is that people work harder for themselves than for others – as with franchising, see Chapter 13. Another is that work is tendered and performed under contract remotely; for example, someone in the next office can be interrupted to attend to a chore, this is more difficult if they are 50 miles away.
- Secretaries play an important role linking remote workers to the company; this provides them with a number of new career opportunities.
- A new flexibility is introduced to people's lives; this may not suit everybody but it certainly avoids the drudgery of commuting. The family unit becomes more significant as all the members can be involved in some way.

This way of working can involve:

- Professional people under contract such as financial and market analysts, public relation specialists and the like. These people work for themselves and provide a service for a fee.
- Professional people working for a salary may be account-

ants, surveyors, computer programmers etc. They are based at home, communicate through a network and generally work on clients' premises.

- Customer service people such as salesmen, service engineers and merchandisers, who have traditionally worked from home and do not need office space. They may be linked by a network.
- Outworkers are people performing regular and routine work who do not necessarily have to be working from a city office. For example, firms supplying financial, technical or property data from records do not necessarily need house analysts, who can work from home and be linked by a network.

There are limitations:

- Not everyone can work for themselves and there are tests to check suitability. However, self-employment is only one of the remote working options.
- The number of managers for every employed remote worker is generally higher than for normal supervision and they need to be of a good calibre. Some people find as much social as financial reward in working together and managers need to balance the benefits of a more flexible working life with some isolation.
- It takes time for any programme to get off the ground because the plan needs to be proven in a pilot scheme before it can be introduced more widely. Six to twelve months should be allowed for testing to prove whether the plan works for all parties.

The sequence of introduction includes: –

- A confidential feasibility study is the necessary first step to work out the potential benefits for both the company and the individual. The analysis should be organised by a senior manager who has the complete backing of the board and he should be supported by an outside specialist who has gained expertise learned elsewhere.
- If the feasibility study is positive a detailed plan needs to be

worked out. This needs to include the working relationship between the parties, the people to be included, the new organisation chart, a likely move to new premises etc. The plan should include contributions from many levels.

- A pilot study is essential for the plan to be tested and acceptable for the people involved. It is wise to start with a few volunteers who have been tested and found suitable for remote working; their practical experience should be fed back into the system before involving others.

Two Important Examples

There are numerous examples of companies that have decided to buy in services or expertise rather than employ staff full time. The importance of Rank Xerox and F International as examples is that they have deliberately set up their own systems for creating or managing independent working. The experience gained by these two companies is explained in more detail in Appendices 11 and 12.

Rank Xerox, the manufacturer of photocopiers, was hit by very serious competition when its patents expired in the late seventies. Urgent action had to be taken to restructure the company and part of the cost saving meant moving the head office away from London. A team was set up under Philip Judkins with the full authority of the board to experiment with a new form of working involving a group of senior staff managers.

The plan aimed to offer managers the opportunity to set up their own companies while still providing their services to the parent. They would appear on the organisation chart and answer to core managers who would be responsible for contracting their services. The first pilot test was undertaken by Roger Walker who provided personnel and training services from a base in Stony Stratford. After several months Walker's experience was shared with people at all levels in the company to introduce a more widely based programme. Over the course of time, over sixty individuals have decided to work in this way with a cost saving to Rank Xerox of over £2.5m.

F International is a remarkable company started by Mrs

Steve Shirley to provide computer programming and related services. Her aim was to mobilise (mainly) female professional programmers who had left full-time employment, usually for family reasons. The company employs around a thousand people of whom only 250 are full-time; the balance of 750 are called the 'panel' and work on a contractual basis for the parent. F International wins contracts which are then performed by the panel working either on clients' premises, at one of the regional offices or at home. Panel members are required to set aside at least twenty-five hours per week of which two days should be spent with the client. F International benefits through considerably lower fixed costs and panel members are able to combine their professional and family lives.

There are four main areas for any company or professional firm to consider:

- The nature of remote working.
- The scope of remote working.
- The ingredients of a successful plan.
- Introducing remote working.

(See also Appendices 11 and 12).

The Nature of Remote Working

Remote working is the process of sub-contracting work to individuals who had been previously in full-time employment. The method of working applies to many categories of staff but excludes those who are necessary to running and directing a business and responsible for its performance.

The prime reason for introducing remote working is to reduce the overheads of employment, and experience shows that one and a half times an individual's salary can be saved by employing similar services through an arms-length contract. Less immediately obvious is the increase in productivity that is generated through personal motivation on the one hand, and more refined operations on the other.

The most immediate change is in the role of parent company managers (called core managers), who need to change their style from being direct supervisors to working with people sited remotely to them. Experience shows that the core manager needs to develop the skill of contract definition, negotiation and management to get the best out of the new contractual relationship. By contrast, the remote workers benefit by developing their abilities to sell and tender their services.

The Scope of Remote Working

Experience shows that there are four basic categories of remote working available to managers who wish to reduce their fixed expenses. These grades vary according to the degree of independence and each needs separate treatment.

Grade 1   Professionals Working Independently
These are individuals who have been working full-time and are given the opportunity to work for themselves. They are thus free to seek other non-competing clients while still providing work for their previous employer. The most important case history comes from Rank Xerox. The company moved their head office from London to Marlow and used the opportunity to reduce their overhead costs by offering a number of their senior executives the chance to become independent while keeping a working relationship.

There is a précis of the Rank Xerox experiment in Appendix 11 which demonstrates the opportunities for cost reduction and some of the skills required for implementation. The categories of professionals who would benefit from a similar approach are:

- Specialised lawyers dealing, for example, with patents.
- Accountants working on financial analysis or on specialised projects.
- Market researchers.
- Public relations specialists.
- Labour relations and training advisers.
- Security and safety advisers.
- Surveyors and architects.
- Stock market, property or other analysts.
- Journalists.

100

Grade 2   *Working Independently but Directed by a Parent*

For professionals who may find it inappropriate, or may not wish, to work independently there is an alternative route that still involves direct supervision by the parent company. The best example is provided by two companies, F International (FI) and Contract Programming Services (CPS).

Both FI and CPS provide programming, systems analysis and computer related services. FI is an independent company that employs full-time 250 out of around 1,000 people to win and manage contracts. The remaining 750 are self-employed individuals working under contract for FI. By contrast, CPS is wholly owned by ICL and all the staff are employees. A précis of both companies is contained in Appendix 12. Professionals suitable for this work are:

- Audit accountants.
- Management consultants.
- Surveyors and assessors.
- Computer programmers, analysts etc.
- Journalists.

Grade 3   *Customer Service*

It is usual for salesmen, service engineers, merchandisers etc to work from their home while in full employment. It is less usual for these individuals to be self-employed in a franchise (see Chapter 13) or in an agency (see Chapter 15).

Grade 4   *Outworking*

Outworking is the description given to important, but repetitious, operations which, for reasons of cost, can be more cheaply carried out remotely. For example, modern methods of networking make it possible for data (such as company accounts) to be summarised and transmitted electronically for central collection. This technique requires a terminal for access to a host computer.

Ingredients of a Successful Plan

This section has been compiled in conjunction with Chamberlains Personnel Services Limited.

FIXED COST REDUCTION, REMOTE WORKING

Introducing remote working, like franchising, needs to benefit both the parent company and the remote worker. In Rank Xerox, for example, the plan was so successful that the number of individuals who initially took up the challenge rose from twelve to sixty over several years. Before introducing the plan the following should be considered:

- Appointment of a change driver to mastermind the project on behalf of the parent company, whose board must provide wholehearted support. He (or she) must be a senior person respected by all levels of management with the personality to see the project to its conclusion.
- Categorise all levels of the company between core management and possible remote workers using the grades given above. This is an essential first stage to evaluate the possibilities both for saving cost and defining different staff categories.
- Consider the implications for the organisation if certain individuals, but not others, are working remotely.
- Contractual relationships defining the position of both parties must be considered at an early stage and these will differ depending on the category of the remote worker. If an individual leaves full-time employment, appropriate redundancy arrangements will need to be agreed and paid before the new relationship can begin.
- Core management training for their new role should be handled by experienced consultants who understand the contractual relationships needed when dealing with remote workers. Training in the use of alternative management styles will also be needed for those supervising independent professional staff.
- The skills and aptitude of all the applicants for remote working will need to be checked by specialists in career counselling techniques; consideration should also be given to counselling spouses and partners.
- Remote workers also need a training programme similar to that of franchisees covering sales, administration, book-keeping etc.
- Network support organisations such as Xanadu were founded to provide important support for new remote

workers. The parent company should consider the option of an existing group or the creation of a new network.

- Cost the programme in terms of redundancy and other payments that will be incurred in implementation. These should include the expense of outside consultants.

Introducing Remote Working

This should be considered in three stages similar to that of franchising.

Stage 1   Feasibility Study
This is a confidential examination which should be carried out by a group of senior managers with the assistance of a consultant to evaluate the potential for remote working. The aim of the study is to provide an overview of the likely costs and savings to cover all aspects of salaries, additional benefits, space occupied and assets such as motor cars and company loans. The benefits would normally include moving to smaller accommodation.

Stage 2   Remote Working Plan
If the results of the feasibility study are positive to both the company and remote workers, all the factors given in the previous section 'Ingredients of a Successful Plan' should be considered. It is important to involve a number of key people who will be concerned both as core managers and remote workers. At this stage volunteers for the pilot study should be carefully screened.

Stage 3   Pilot Study
Unlike a franchise pilot study (when an individual will be entering a tried system) the first remote worker will be developing and proving the system as he or she proceeds. It is essential that the correct core manager be appointed because this will be as much a test for the company as for the remote worker. It would be wise not to proceed with the second pilot study unless both parties are satisfied with the formula.

15
Fixed Cost Reduction Through Agency Working

This chapter completes the examination of methods available to reduce costs without diminishing efficiency. Agency representation is not at present in wide use, but it is an essential tool available to sales directors in the event of a downturn in business. A skilled sales force represents a fixed cost of around 15 per cent of sales revenues, compared with the variable costs of agency commissions averaging up to 10 per cent. This is a saving of one-third and a useful reduction of the break-even point.

Agency working has a considerable history; there are a number of instances in the USA where good salesmen have left full-time employment to join an agency or become independent. However, the movement is not widespread and the aim of this chapter is to identify the present trends of sales-force management and to show how agency working can be introduced for operational or cost-cutting reasons.

There are five sections:

- Trends of sales management.
- Principles of agency working.
- An example of converting employees to independence.
- Essential features of conversion.
- Introducing agency working.

(See also Appendices 13 and 14).

Trends in Sales Management

Managing a sales force has become more professional and has encouraged outside agencies to supply support services such as tele-sales and specialised software.

- There is a general trend for sales forces to become smaller, more highly trained, better motivated and less inclined to change employment. In financial services, however, the size of the sales force is increasing.
- Tele-sales techniques are being used increasingly to make appointments, conduct market surveys and to generate follow-up orders. Telephone selling is overtaking direct mail as the most widely used method of promotion and there is a growth of specialised agencies available to make surveys or conduct campaigns.
- Sales management is being supported by a wide range of software and networking programmes. Typically these are used for recording information, preparing reports, prompting calls and preparing questions.
- Specialist services such as merchandising are brought in where these are not provided.

Principles of Agency Working

The growth of agency representation – particularly in the USA – has shown that fixed costs of direct selling can be converted to the variable costs of commissions. Agency selling allows principals to follow a flexible sales strategy; for example, agencies might promote to smaller customers while using direct selling to major accounts. The most important features are set out below with a more detailed description in Appendix 13.

- Salesmen have achieved independence by using their skills to represent several non-competing principals. Coverage is extensive and one of the largest agency associations lists over ninety member industries.
- Territories are usually confined to states adjacent to the agency's head office although some of the larger specialist firms are national. Coverage is often extended by arranging affiliations with non-competitive agents in other areas.
- Agency representation can often be combined with direct selling where this can be organised without conflict. For example, agencies may be used for selling

to distributors while direct salesmen promote to original equipment accounts.

- Agencies are paid by commission on net invoiced sales, making it possible for a principal to open accounts in a new area more cheaply than through direct selling. Agency working is particularly attractive to importers.
- Many agencies are formed by employees often with the encouragement of previous employers. Principals need a different management style when dealing with associates rather than subordinates.
- Agency agreements should be carefully considered by both parties to avoid subsequent misunderstandings. Agency associations promote member concerns and provide sample forms to help draft agreements.
- Consumer agency selling is growing for personal items such as cosmetics, clothes and jewellery. The range has been increased to houseware items including cleaners, cookware, curtains and ceramics. Personal selling has been particularly successful where merchandise can be demonstrated and recommended from personal experience.

An Example of Converting Employees to Independence

It is often hard for an employee to change from employed security to independence; the transition is also difficult for many managements who dislike losing direct operational control. In an agency arrangement the employer becomes a principal who relies on agents for generating sales. Employees become independent, relying on commission for remuneration and taking responsibility for all aspects of running their own business.

One example of conversion from employee to independence is the milk round in Britain. Milk has been traditionally delivered to the door by milkmen employed by dairies. Competition from supermarkets and changing patterns of employment reduced the demand for delivered milk. A milk round is costly to organise and dairy management sought alternative means of maintaining volume and reducing costs. One answer was to induce milkmen to become independent

16

Finding Out What you Don't Know from What You Do

This chapter is primarily written for those shareholders, suppliers, lenders, professional advisers or customers who may wish to assess future relationships with a business, yet have only published information available. The chapter aims to provide a set of signposts enabling the reader to come to an independent view of future relationships. To avoid numerous cross-references, some of the material is duplicated from other parts of the book.

The Chinese have a game called 'stone, scissors, paper' which is usually played between two people. The players make two strokes of the hand in unison before making the shape of a stone (clenched fist), scissors (two fingers extended like scissor blades) or paper (hand outstretched). Stone blunts scissors, paper covers stone and scissors cut paper. Each individual game is won by correctly anticipating the other's next move by analysing what has gone before.

Judging the likely outcome from management decisions, in particular circumstances, is similar to playing the Chinese game. The observer knows the past track record from previous financial results and can make a good guess at management strategy for any particular stage in the business cycle. By putting these two together a shrewd judgement can be made as to the company continuing to be a good investment, client, borrower or trading partner in the future. This approach is not confined to companies; in sport, good team managers take endless trouble to study opposition tactics in order to guess how they are likely to play on the day.

Good generals do the same and it is no accident that the chapter heading is taken from the Duke of Wellington's celebrated quotation:

all the business of war, and indeed all the business of life, is to endeavour to find out what you don't know from what you do; that is what I called guessing what was at the other side of the hill.
(Croker Papers, 1885)

The board of a company has to make two fundamental decisions. The first is to devise a commercial strategy that reflects external opportunities (or constraints) within the business cycle; for example, it makes sense to grow through acquisition when a business cycle is in full flood. It becomes progressively risky to take the same action towards the end of the cycle.

The second decision concerns risks with the balance sheet; it could be wise to increase debt at the beginning of a cycle, knowing that this could be funded by a rights issue. It would be folly to take the same action during a bear market.

This chapter examines the problem under four headings.

- Measuring a company's financial track record.
- Judging the position in the business cycle.
- Taking a view on board policy.
- Coming to a judgement.

Measuring a Company's Financial Track Record

There are several ways of measuring a board's financial track record, probably the easiest being the Z-score system which shows present and past performance in a single figure. A more detailed account of solvency-measuring methods is to be found in Appendix 5.

The Z-score was first developed by Professor Edward Altman of New York University and explained in his book *Corporate Bankruptcy in America*. Altman used a technique known as multiple discriminant analysis, to examine and weigh the most significant financial ratios that distinguished between previous failed and healthy companies. When a company had a Z-score below a certain threshold it was at risk of failure; when above, there was very little chance of problems for the coming year.

114

WHAT YOU DON'T KNOW FROM WHAT YOU DO

Professor Richard Taffler of the City University Business School extended Altman's work in Britain in two significant ways. Firstly, he ranked the Z-score with others out of 100 to derive a percentile – or PAS-score – which could be plotted; secondly, he ranked each ratio with others on the data base to direct the analyst towards the most significant areas in the company accounts. Fig 20 in Appendix 5 shows an example of both the graph – known as the trajectory – and the ratio analysis for Rotaprint plc, a company that failed in February 1988.

Judging the Position in the Business Cycle

Since World War II, the average business cycle, as defined by rise and fall of interest rates in the USA, has lasted around seven years. The interest rates are defined by the yield of the US thirty-year Treasury Bond and ninety-day Treasury Bill regularly reported in the financial press. A record of the four cycles is shown in Appendix 1 which also includes the yield curve, ie the T-bond yield minus the T-bill yield. Historically, the negative movement of the yield curve has been a very important pre-indicator of financial crises and recessions. A more detailed account of business cycles is contained in Chapter 2.

At the beginning of a cycle the T-bill yield drops below that of the T-bond, thus making the yield curve positive; at the end of the cycle the position reverses and the yield curve goes negative.

The curve can be divided into three stages: coming out of recession; mid-term; and inflation and beyond. These last roughly two, three and a half and one and a half years respectively. During the first two stages, managers can, and often do, take risks which are very successful. Even if they fail, it may be possible to recover the position with a rights issue or the business may be sold. The same risks taken during the third phase may be terminal. Observers should therefore measure when the yield curve became (or becomes) positive, then judge for themselves the present position within the business cycle.

Taking a View on Board Policy

The next step is to match a board's business policy, as demonstrated by their decisions, to the three stages of the business cycle considered in the previous section and in Chapter 2.

Stage 1   Coming Out of a Recession

Although not perfectly regular, the signal for the ending of post-war recessions occurred in 1961, 1968 (confused somewhat by the Vietnam War), 1975 and 1982. During each period, short-term interest rates were low or declining and the yield curve was becoming positive. The pattern together with appropriate management action is suggested in Fig 12.

Indicators	Implications	Investments	Business strategy
Bond yields start to rise	Recession ending	Stocks	Negotiate long-term supply
Stock Market decline arrested	Unemployment static	Real estate	Favourable long-term investment
	Inventories minimum		
Yield curve positive	Interest rates low		Management style changes
	High failure rates		Protect receivables
Commodities stop falling	Tariffs falling		Renegotiate sales contract
			New labour contracts

Fig. 12   Policy planning for start of business cycle

Stage 2   Mid-term

After two years of government-sponsored growth, most managements become more optimistic about the future and the stock market will be responding to improved profitability and low interest rates. The optimism will be shown in reduced unemployment and greater investment (see Fig 13).

Indicators	Implications	Investment	Business strategy
Bill yield below bond yields	Unemployment starts falling	Stocks Real estate	Acquisitions made through loans – later rights issues
Positive yield curve	Interest rates rise gently		Invest for productivity
Stock market rises	Out of recession		Increase prices with inflation

Fig. 13   Policy planning for mid-term

Stage 3   Inflation and Beyond

After around five and a half to six years from the yield curve becoming positive, there will be tell-tale signs that the dangerous Stage 3 is starting. The first indication is a rise in interest rates; next, debt levels will rise and the financial institutions will be bombarding the public with even more ingenious ways of borrowing money. All these are signs of potential inflation which historically has led to even higher rates, a financial crisis and finally a recession. There are three phases:

Phase 1   Inflation

The most important indicators are commodities; these reflect a movement out of paper assets into physical investments such as raw materials. One of the most significant indicators is the US Commodity Research Bureau (CRB) index calculated from a basket of commodities; another indicator is the Reuters Commodity Index.

Fig 14 shows the most significant factors and the proposed investment and business strategy for this phase. Alert managements will be taking steps to eliminate debt, and making long-term plans to reduce costs.

Phase 2   Crisis

The first phase culminates in a steep rise in commodity prices and interest rates before an equally steep fall. Management who read the signs correctly will be cash rich and investing for a recession; they will not be taking commercial

Indicators	Implications	Investments	Business strategy
CRB Index rising	Growth continues	Watch for stocks to peak	Prepare cover plan for up to 25 per cent reduction in volume/prices
T-Bond yields rising	Profits increase	Bonds bearish	
CPI rises	Real estate prices boom	Buy resource-based stocks and precious metals	Avoid new onerous leases and commitments
Interest rates become negative	Pre-election political response		Categorise subsidiaries into 'holds' and 'sells'. Arrange disposal of sells
			Update plans for protection of receivables
			Introduce plans for remote working or franchising
			Consider alternative plans for financing of inventory & its control
			Consider forward sales contract at fixed prices
			Invest in cost reduction facilities
			Sell surplus real estate
			Management training in new skills

Fig. 14   Policy planning for inflation

risks or extending their balance sheet (See Fig 15).

Phase 3   Decline

Historically, a 'spike' in interest rates has always been followed by a steep decline and a fall in commodity prices; companies that have failed to take precautions will be scrambling for liquidity. These are dangerous times for the

Indicators	Implications	Investments	Business Strategy
CRB peaks	Growth peaks	Switch to cash	Pay off debts and become cash rich
T-bond yields rising	US federal deficit rises (⅔ CPI related)	Avoid risky deposits	Introduce cost reduction programme
T-bill yields rising	'Hot' money leaves	At peak, start to invest in fixed interest stocks	Maximum protection of receivable minimum inventory investment
CPI rises	Real estate starts to fall	Sell precious metals	
Yield curve becomes negative			Introduce new management programmes
Interest rates 'spike'			Appoint sub-contractors and check continuity
			Avoid new purchase commitments, negotiate away liabilities
			Introduce personnel programmes for cost reduction

Fig. 15   Policy planning for crisis

overborrowed and the beginning of corporate failures (See Fig 16).

Coming to a Judgement

This section is written in the form of a checklist aimed to help the analyst to compare company reports against financial performance and the state of the business cycle. If board policy is out of line with what has been regarded as prudent in the past, it is an opportunity to make more detailed enquiries and, if necessary, to alter the relationship. The headings are the same as those in the previous section 'Taking a View on Board Policy'.

Stage 1   Coming Out of Recession
This is a cautionary period when bad news is more likely

Indicators	Implications	Investments	Business strategy
CRB falls	Rapid decline in growth	Investment in fixed interest and cash at call	After initial panic, adjust business to declining volumes
Interest rates rapid fall but secondary spike in 1991	Government forced to retrench	Seek 'trades' in stock market during rallies	Invest in new service type operation to maintain assets, ie cars, homes, household goods
CPI falls	Support for home finance, workforce programme widespread	Devise gold % fixed interest strategy for secondary rally in yields	Use of franchising
T-bond and T-bill yields fall but secondary rise later			Vigilance for failures
	Tariffs start losing around trading blocs		Seek opportunities for selective investments in companies or assets
	Real estate values fall		Invest heavily in marketing and innovations
			Reduce production liabilities
			Product life cycles reduced

Fig. 16   Policy planning for recession

to be believed than good. However, a judgement about a board's strategy may be formed through press reports, direct business contacts or by pertinent questioning on occasions such as an AGM.

1 Expected duration: around two years from when the yield curve becomes positive.
2 Expected Z-score movement: positive from a low base as business improves and margins strengthen. However, watch for negative movements which would give clues to overtrading.
3 Management action: would be cautious with investment being made into replacement, not new capacity. Be cautious about bold new initiatives launched from a weak balance sheet. Identify those companies that were taking steps to replace the previous management with a more aggressive entrepreneurial style.

Stage 2   Mid-term

This is the time for picking winners by the style of management. Aggressive leaders will be identified by their efficiency in executing expansion, particularly acquisitions. There will be failures from management expanding too rapidly from a weak cash-flow position (it is a form of overtrading called 'flywheeling' where the rate of expansion is just slower than the increase in interest rates – see Chapter 1).

- Expected duration: about three and a half years.
- Expected Z-score movement: increasingly positive, some companies spectacularly so.
- Management action is becoming bolder as confidence increases and risks are taken that would not have been contemplated previously. Watch for the 'new breed' of aggressive entrepreneurs who will gain a big following from highly leveraged take-over moves. Investment plans will be expansionary and a number of cross-border acquisitions will be made.

Outsiders should still be cautious of major expansion made on thin balance sheets. Risk-takers may succeed but most will be acquired and a few will fail.

Stage 3   Inflation and Beyond

It is important to divide this potentially dangerous stage into the three phases already discussed; however, it is not easy to be precise about the boundaries. The first importance is for management to understand that they have only a relatively short time to pay off debt and reduce costs.

- Expected duration: around one and a half years to the end of the interest rate 'spike'.
- Expected Z-score movement. This will lag behind events because of the delay in publishing accounts; however, it would be foolhardy not to be concerned about companies either at risk of financial distress or those with a declining and low trajectory.
- Management action should be primarily concerned with

121

reducing debt and fixed costs during Phase 1 (the inflationary phase) in anticipation on Phases 2 and 3. Fortunately, the positive steps are usually reported and the outside observer should expect to see the following:

- Sales of excess property or other assets.
- Negotiated management buy-outs for subsidiaries.
- Reduced headquarters staff and move to smaller premises.
- Negotiated flexible arrangements to convert short- to long-term debt and rights issues.
- Rationalisation measures that increase output per person and reduce costs.

Negative steps that will increase risks are:

- Acquisitions made by increasing borrowings.
- Expanding on a weak balance sheet.
- Embarking on a major diversification.

APPENDICES

1

What the Economic Cycles Mean for Business

Since World War II, the free world has been strongly influenced by political and economic events in the USA and it is likely that this will continue for several years. Despite budget and trade deficits, America is still the world's largest economy and the impact of her political decisions is widespread.

This appendix provides background detail to Chapters 2 and 16, describing appropriate management action at each stage of the business cycle and how these may be judged. There are three headings:

- The lessons of previous cycles.
- Leading indicators.
- Historical comparisons.

The Lessons of Previous Cycles

The following sections provide a conducted tour of the business cycles since World War I and their significance for the present.

Expectation of Inflation or Deflation – Chart 4

Cycles almost invariably end with a burst of inflation so the first task is to judge the long-term trend of deflation or inflation. This is illustrated in Chart 4, marking the trend of the US long-term bond yield.

The US Government funds its spending programme by issuing securities through an auction. As with many countries, the bills and bonds have varying redemption maturities which range from months to decades. At the long end of the market, the security known as the Treasury Bond (T-Bond)

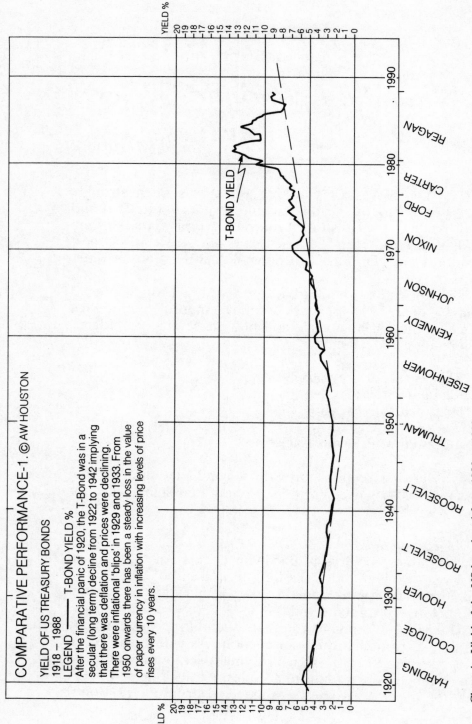

COMPARATIVE PERFORMANCE-1. © AW HOUSTON

YIELD OF US TREASURY BONDS
1918 – 1988
LEGEND ———— T-BOND YIELD %
After the financial panic of 1920, the T-Bond was in a
secular (long term) decline from 1922 to 1942 implying
that there was deflation and prices were declining.
There were inflational 'blips' in 1929 and 1933. From
1950 onwards there has been a steady loss in the value
of paper currency in inflation with increasing levels of price
rises every 10 years.

T-BOND YIELD

Chart 4   Yield of the US long bond from 1920 to 1989

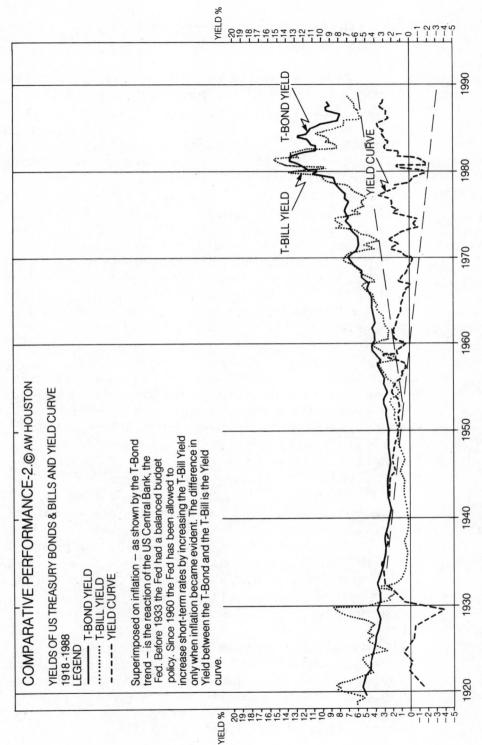

Chart 5   Yields of the US Treasury Bond, Treasury Bill and Yield Curve

has a maturity of thirty years. Once issued, the bond is held by investors and its price depends upon the expected rate of inflation. If lower inflation is anticipated (implying a rise in the value of money) the yield reduces; if higher, the yield rises.

From 1920 to the early forties the yield was in steady decline, indicating lower inflation; however, there were exceptions. There was a financial panic in 1920 which increased the rates, and inflation about the time of the 1929 Wall Street Crash and a further rise in the yield during the 1933 banking crisis. From about 1950, however, the value of money has fallen as shown by the steady increase in the bond yield. Superimposed on the rise there have been bursts of extra inflation every seven or ten years; these have risen progressively from 1960 through to the last crisis in 1980. Each time the yield has touched the trend line after a fall, there has been the expectation of a new inflationary cycle.

The Response of the US Government to Inflation – Chart 5

Chart 5 shows how the authorities have responded to inflation by altering the yield of the Treasury Bill (T-Bill). The T-Bill is one of the important instruments for regulating the supply of money into the banking system. When the Federal Reserve Bank (Fed) judges that credit should be eased, the bill yield is lowered. When money needs to be removed from the system, the Fed bids a higher yield.

From 1920 to 1930, the Fed was restricting the amount of money into the banking system and the T-Bill yield was almost consistently above that of the T-Bond. From 1931 onwards, there was such anxiety to overcome the recession that T-Bill yields were bid down, to below 0.1 per cent in 1937. From 1950 onwards, however, the Fed has tracked the bond yield by increasing the bill yield whenever inflation was deemed to be excessive and released rates as soon as economically possible.

Finally, the yield curve line on the chart shows the difference between the bond and bill yield. When the yield curve is positive, it implies that the authorities wish to increase the supply of credit to the economy; when negative, it is restrictive. Since 1950 the yield curve has been a very important factor for judging the state of the economic cycle.

The Importance of the Yield Curve – Chart 6

Chart 6 shows how the authorities use the yield curve to control the US economy and hence influence the free world. It also has an important influence on the Stock Market, on housebuilding and many other industries.

Recessions are heavily correlated with the yield curve and in many cases coincide with the first year of a new presidency. It seems that outgoing presidents try to keep the economy going until the next election, leaving the successor to take remedial action (see Chart 4). The solution to excessive credit is to increase the T-Bill yield and push the yield curve negative; this in turn has a dramatic impact on economic expectations.

Housebuilding is but one of the sectors that correlates strikingly with the yield curve. The first example was in the twenties when the negative yield curve reduced housebuilding by nearly 90 per cent. Since 1970, the decline and recovery have coincided precisely with the yield curve becoming negative and positive respectively.

Stock markets have closely followed the yield curve. The only bear markets not accompanied by a negative yield curve were in 1937, 1962 and 1987. Conversely, every bull market since World War II was resignalled by the yield curve becoming positive.

The Rise in Credit Since World War II – Chart 7

The most striking factor in the post-war years is the exponential rise in credit created by the Fed, shown in Chart 7. Up to World War II, the total credit created by the Fed was in the order of $4bn which was expanded to $24bn in 1942 where it remained until the fifties.

Since around 1955 there has been a steady expansion in the quantity of notes issued (the largest proportion of Federal credit). Increased credit has enabled the authorities to keep interest rates low except when inflation became excessive. It is of interest that every seven years from 1953, the rise in interest rates has just gone through the exponential curve, suggesting that the next peak in rates should be well over 20 per cent.

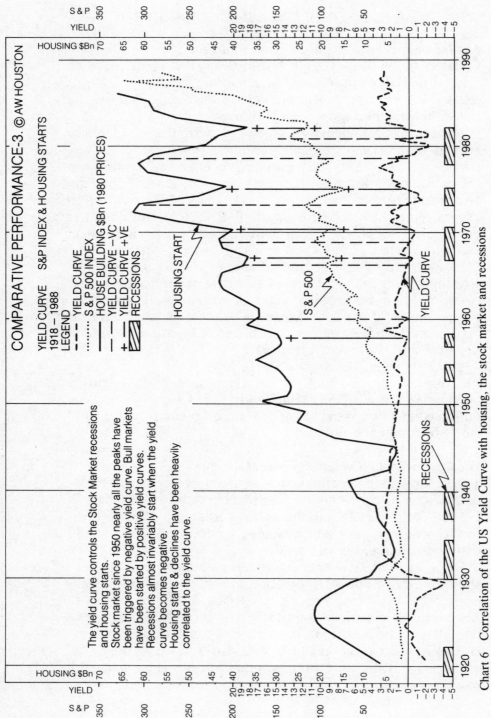

COMPARATIVE PERFORMANCE-3. © AW HOUSTON

YIELD CURVE   S&P INDEX & HOUSING STARTS
1918 – 1988
LEGEND
--- YIELD CURVE
··· S & P 500 INDEX
— HOUSE BUILDING $Bn (1980 PRICES)
— YIELD CURVE –VC
+ YIELD CURVE +VE
▨ RECESSIONS

The yield curve controls the Stock Market recessions
and housing starts.
Stock market since 1950 nearly all the peaks have
been triggered by negative yield curve. Bull markets
have been started by positive yield curves.
Recessions almost invariably start when the yield
curve becomes negative.
Housing starts & declines have been heavily
correlated to the yield curve.

HOUSING START

S & P 500

YIELD CURVE

RECESSIONS

Chart 6   Correlation of the US Yield Curve with housing, the stock market and recessions

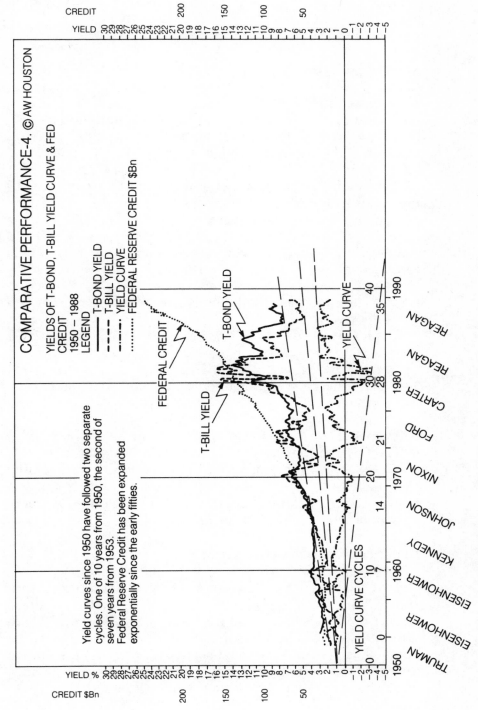

Chart 7   US T-Bond, T-Bill, Yield Curve and Federal Credit since 1950

Leading Indicators

When excessive credit is created, it can either move into financial assets (as in 1929 and 1987) or physical assets such as commodities (as in 1974 and 1980).

Commodities are a leading indicator for inflation as they cover a span of precious metals, base metals and soft crops ranging from rubber through to sugar and wheat. The additional demand created by inflation bids up the price of commodities, their rise being followed, in about three to five months, by an increase in yields.

One of the most widely used commodity indices is the CRB index (Commodity Research Bureau). The CRB is a weighted average of a number of commodities with a bias to crops and is quoted daily in the *Wall Street Journal*. The Reuters Commodity Index is another yardstick; it has a bias towards non-ferrous metals and is quoted daily in the *Financial Times*.

Readers who wish to follow the stages in a business cycle should watch indicators available from the financial press or commodity brokers. Individual requirements will define which are the most significant, but the following should be included:

- The yields of the T-Bond and T-Bill, also the yield curve.
- The CRB index and some other commodity such as gold.
- The major currencies, ie yen, D-mark and sterling related to the US $.
- The major stock market indicators, Dow Jones Average, Nikkei Dow and Financial Times Index.

Historical Comparisons – Chart 8

One of the most important similarities between the present and the thirties is the accumulation of US debt measured against the Gross National Product (GNP). By mid-1988 the ratio was only 12 per cent below the peak of 1930. These debt levels are unlikely to be sustained. Only a small move towards recession places a strain upon illiquid debtors; once these try to pay off debt, there is a huge liquidation of assets creating a 'spike' in interest rates.

After 1931 both the GNP and debt declined. Over four years, from 1930 to 1934, the GNP nearly halved and credit fell by around 30 per cent.

DEBT*-TO-GNP: 1920-1987

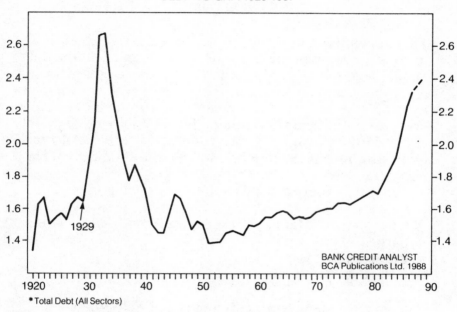

* Total Debt (All Sectors)

Chart 8   Debt to GNP ratio in the US from 1920 to 1987

133

2

Turning Assets Into Cash

This appendix is designed to be read with Chapter 3, the restorative programme of reducing costs and funding debt. Selling assets is a painful process because many managers regard it as an admission of failure; even worse is the need to sell a company that has recently been purchased. However, do not despair of finding a buyer. Many more people are seeking to own their own firms and it is easier to raise money to buy an existing business than to find capital for a new enterprise.

Chapter 3 grouped disposals into three categories:

- Category 1   Management buy-outs and sales to third parties.
- Category 2   Asset sales.
- Category 3   Closure.

Category 1   Management Buy-outs and Sales to Third Parties

This section describes how to sell an existing business, either to the management through a buy-out or to a third party; in each case, the preparation for sale is similar. This section has been compiled with the help of Investors In Industry (3is).

During the eighties there has been an increasing willingness amongst management to seek independence by owning their companies. In 1988, for example, Britain had a higher pool of capital available for ventures per Gross National Product (GNP) than the USA. Of the £700m generated in 1987, 45 per cent was mobilised to help management teams buy their own businesses.

There are a number of reasons why parent companies may wish to sell their subsidiaries:

- Cash is required to fund debt: the prime requirement of the survival plan.
- The subsidiary is not a core activity and therefore becomes a 'sell' category.
- It is an unwanted part of an acquisition.
- It will not be earning the required return on capital in the foreseeable future.
- Funds or management effort would be better deployed elsewhere in the group.
- If the vendor is a family company, the owners may wish to raise cash and invest elsewhere.

Management Buy-Out v Sale to a Third Party

During periods of growth, a vendor can often get a better price by selling the business to a trading entity than through a buy-out. However, there are a number of factors that should be taken into account before the decision is made:

- The managers are essential to the continuation of the business and may make a sale difficult should they not accept the proposed new owners.
- It is almost impossible to keep an offer for sale confidential thus giving competitors a commercial advantage.
- Warranties and indemnities may be kept to a minimum in concluding a buy-out negotiation.
- There can be a continuity of relationship between the vendor, new shareholders, customers and suppliers in a buy-out. This is often not possible with a third-party sale.
- It is most likely that employees will relate better to owner managers than to a group, especially when they are themselves shareholders.
- There can be considerable gains for vendor management who are seen to offer former employees a chance to own their own business.
- Investors who support a management buy-out benefit from being shareholders in a business with a sharp market or product focus.
- The reduced formalities speed up the buy-out process and completion is often more rapid than for a trade sale.

Preparing a Business for Disposal

There are a number of venture capitalists who are capable of assembling investors for a company buy-out. It is essential, however, that both parties are first convinced that the management team can deliver the expected results.

The most important document for the venture capitalist is the business plan, which can combine the expertise of the vendor group with the knowledge of the local management. Where outside investors are involved, the assumptions made in the projections will need to be checked by financial specialists.

The business plan should include:

- The objectives of the buy-out team.
- Business profiles of the management team, their length of service and track record in their present responsibility. There should also be a management chart showing the team after the buy-out, clearly indicating the leader.
- A description of the business, several years financial accounts and the record of previous performance.
- A description of the products or services in comparison with the competition and the steps that are being taken to retain and develop the present position.
- The market profile of the business to show the degree of sales penetration, the spread of sales accounts and methods of promotion.
- A description of the productive or service process and the major resource items.
- A chart of the present organisation pinpointing the key individuals. This should include a description of each department and its ability to work as a unit – independent of the previous parent.
- The most recent report and accounts with up-to-date valuations on items such as property, ownership of significant assets and potential claims or liabilities.
- Future business strategy and financial projections. It is most important that these follow naturally from past performance and any assumptions should be included.
- The effect of the financial projections on the cash flow and the impact of not achieving the forecast results.
- Capital requirements.

136

Ownership of an Independent Company

It is the practice of venture capitalists to look for the management of newly independent companies to have committed a
major part of their own assets to the venture. They should
suffer loss if things go wrong or gain if successful. In times of
growth, this objective has been reached through a high level
of personal borrowing at a fixed rate of interest and corporate
overdraft at variable rates. There is also the expectation that a
capital gain will be realised through widening the share ownership at some time in the future.

It would be most unwise to undertake a high level of
gearing at the end of a business cycle and venture capitalists would seek their return more from income than capital
appreciation. In these circumstances, investors would seek
to encourage management through the issue of redeemable
shares. Depending upon performance, the directors would
claim a higher proportion of the remaining shareholding
once the redeemable share holdings had been bought by the
outside shareholders.

Category 2 Asset Sales

A buy-out is unlikely to work for an item of plant or an activity
that could only exist as part of a larger group; for example,
sales of a product that could only be made from specialised
machinery. However, it is still possible to obtain reasonable
value for the asset and, in order to attract the right buyer, it is
wise to prepare a prospectus detailing the following:

- Several years' sales and gross margin comparisons.
- List of the major customers and their offtake.
- Description of the machinery, its age, serviceability, pro-
  vision of spares, etc.
- List of key personnel who can either be employed by the
  purchaser or used for specialised training.
- List of key component suppliers (if any).

Seeking Buyers

Once details have been prepared, the most likely buyers will
be competitors although this risks downgrading the product

in the eyes of customers. A less hazardous approach, although more expensive, is to seek a buyer from overseas. The major problem will be keeping customers while finding a buyer because it is highly uneconomical to continue production. One possible solution is to maintain deliveries from a foreign supplier.

Selling Assets to Present Customers

It may be possible to sell plant to a customer where there is a strong negotiating position through the ownership of specialist plant or tooling. In this case a smooth transfer can be organised with the maximum of goodwill.

Category 3   Closure

The list of sells will almost inevitably include those activities that are no longer commercial and should be closed. This is a painful process which leads to staff redundancies and a write-down of assets. However, do not delay the decision through fear of the consequences; any postponement will lead to further losses and the people concerned may be penalised in finding new jobs. Implementation should include the following:

- List all the people who will be made redundant and establish the precise statutory requirement for their dismissal. There may also be a company policy for additional payments that have been agreed previously.
- List all the surplus assets, their open-market value and the likely write-down.
- The closure timetable will depend upon completing work for customers. This may include phasing the run-down and transferring work elsewhere. Avoid this, it is expensive.
- When a programme has been agreed, be careful in phasing announcements, as nothing is worse than dealing with rumours that cannot be denied. On the day, inform all concerned, employees, customers, suppliers, the local press etc in such a way as to avoid uncertainty and distress wherever possible.

3
Aide-Memoire for Negotiations

Towards the end of a business cycle (defined in Chapter 2, Stage 3) it is important to create the maximum flexibility for manoeuvre. This is particularly important when negotiating long-term supply or property leases which could prove burdensome in the event of a business downturn or if things went wrong.

This appendix is designed as an *aide-memoire* when negotiating heads of agreement and has been compiled with the assistance of Taylor Garrett. There are five sections:

- Factors for consideration.
- Property leases.
- Contracts of employment.
- Long-term contracts.
- Preparing a business for sale.

Factors for Consideration

Long-term contracts may be either beneficial or onerous and their success depends upon whether assumptions made during negotiations prove correct. For example, a long-term sales contract for the supply of material to a major account at an agreed price would be highly beneficial to the supplier in the event of a drop in purchase values. Conversely, a company signing a twenty-five year lease for an expensive office suite just before a decline in demand (for accommodation) would be severely embarrassed. This appendix takes the position of the disadvantaged party.

The following are general factors that would apply to most contracts:

- Reduce the duration of a contract so that the terms can be renegotiated if the economic climate changes for the worse. Long-term contracts can be negotiated with some confidence at the beginning of an economic cycle; it is folly to make an onerous long-term contract at the end of a cycle.

- Avoid giving collateral that does not expire on the termination of a contract. For example, it is unwise to give a property lease guarantee (often required from directors of a smaller company) that does not end with the lease.
- Arrange for a lease that is capable of being sub-let at a lower rent without a penalty being applied by the landlord. This is particularly important where less space is needed than was first thought.
- Convert fixed to variable costs where possible in order to reduce the break-even point. The aim is to reduce the duration of any fixed-cost contract – possibly by increasing bonuses for performance.
- Introduce *force majeure* clauses where possible so that the contract is void or modified in certain conditions. For example, interest rates rising above 15 per cent, inflation increasing above 10 per cent or the stock market falling more than 500 points.
- Avoid cross-guarantees which are often required by banks or property lessors. These reduce flexibility and give rise to contingent liabilities over a longer period. Assets or companies will be easier to sell when these are unencumbered by cross-guarantees.
- Flexibility is increased if liabilities are contracted at the operating level. To achieve this, it may be necessary to divide large concentrations of assets into separate companies.

Property Leases

A modern lease for new property in the UK is likely to be for twenty-five years, with (upward only) rent reviews every five years. This may prove uneconomic if demand for space or rental values decline. The following are points for consideration in relation to property leases:

- Avoid the 'upward only' clause where possible.
- Seek shorter rent review intervals where it is believed that rental levels will decline.
- Seek the right to sub-let without consent where less space will be needed than was first thought.
- Consider a *force majeure* clause with the landlord, allowing a lower rental to be negotiated at the review date if there is a specified difference between market and the existing rates.
- Avoid giving parent company guarantees for subsidiary companies.
- Arrange that the landlord cannot reasonably withhold permission for a lease to be assigned to another tenant. Nevertheless, the original tenant will remain liable in the event of failure.
- Limit repairing covenants to a position that may be negotiated at the termination of a lease.

Note Cash-rich lessees may buy back property from the landlord if values fall to a level where the avoidance of present rents would be a sound return on investment.

Contracts of Employment

The primary objective for an employer is to convert fixed into variable costs and to limit the duration of employment contracts. To achieve this, introduce as large a bonus element as reasonable into the employment benefits and make others available such as pension portability and share options. The bonus element should apply to pension, insurance and other entitlements.

Long-term Contracts

See 'Factors for Consideration' already described. The position depends upon being at an advantage or disadvantage in the changed circumstances.

Preparing a Business for Sale

Companies are most easily sold when they are free of burdensome contracts. Warranties are almost always required by the purchaser which promotes disclosure of possible liabilities and may lead to an adjustment in the purchase consideration. Warranties are limited in a management buy-out as it is assumed that management is already aware of the pitfalls.

4

Examples of Hedging Currency and Interest Rate Risks

Example of Hedging Currency Risks
Reprinted from an Introduction to LIFFE

A Fixed Hedge
A UK exporter expects to receive $2.5 million in December 1987 for a large machine tool order. The current sterling spot rate in October is $1.6500, the LIFFE futures rate for December delivery is $1.6520, and the LIFFE Sterling December call option with a $1.65 exercise price is selling for 4.00¢.

Option contract size = £25,000

Equivalent at $1.65 to $41,250

$$\text{Number of contracts for total hedge} = \frac{\$2,500,000}{\$41,250} = 61 \text{ contracts}$$

Buy 61 December $1.65 calls

Cost of option   = 61 × £25,000
                     = $61,000 (ie 2.4% of expected
                                receipts)

December 15

Scenario 1

December 1987 Dollar-Sterling rate $1.75
$1.65 Call Option premium = 10.10¢

(a) Exporter sells $2.5 million at spot rate of $1.75
     Proceeds = £1,428,571

(b) Exporter sells 61 December $1.65 calls at 10.10¢
    Options Profit = 61 × £25,000 × ($0.1010–$0.04)
                   = $93,025
    Equivalent at $1.75 to £53,157.14

$$\frac{£2,500,000}{£1,428,571 + £53,157.14}$$

$$= \$1.6872$$

This may be compared with the original futures rate of $1.6520 in October. The option purchaser has been protected against the fall in value of his dollar receipts, at a cost which is slightly less than the original cost of the option, ie 4.00¢.

Scenario 2

December 1987 Dollar-Sterling rate $1.55
$1.65 Call Option premium = 0.0¢

(a) Exporter sells $2,500,000 at spot rate of $1.55
    Proceeds = £1,612,903

(b) Options expire worthless

    Equivalent at $1.55 to £39,354.84

(c) Effective exchange rate = $$\frac{\$2,500,000}{£1,612,903 - £39,354.84}$$

$$= \$1.5888$$

Again this may be compared with the original futures rate of $1.6520.

The options purchaser has in this case gained through the rise in value of his dollar receipts at the cost of only the original price of the option.

As expected if the exchange rate moves in the unanticipated unfavourable direction, the forward or futures exchange rate will produce a better effective exchange rate. The options hedge does preserve some of the benefits of a favourable exchange rate movement. But now suppose the exporter was not certain that he would receive the order. If he did not receive the dollar payment, then the result of his futures/options positions would be:

	Rate = $1.55	Rate = $1.75
Futures Hedge	Loss = $155,550	Gain = $149,450
Options Hedge	Loss = $61,000	Gain = $93,025

Although the windfall gained for a rise in the exchange rate is larger with the futures hedge, the potential loss for a decline in the exchange rate is unlimited with the futures hedge and limited to $61,000 for the options hedge. For uncertain cash flows, the options hedge will certainly therefore be less risky and is likely to be preferred.

Example of Hedging Interest Rate Risks

A Borrower

It is 1 February. A borrower has a £500,000 three-month loan from the money market at a rate of 10 per cent which is due to be rolled over on 31 May. The borrower is worried that rates will have risen by then.

The borrower decides to use LIFFE's Three-Month Sterling Interest Rate contract to cover the risk of higher interest rates. The contract is for a three-month deposit facility of £500,000 beginning in March, June, September or December. The borrower selects the June delivery month as the March contract will have matured before the 31 May rollover.

The contract is priced by deducting the deposit interest rate from 100.00. On 1 February the interest rate is 10 per cent and the price of the contract accordingly is 90.00. The price of the contract changes up and down in minimum amounts of 0.01 known as 'ticks'. The value of each tick is:

145

0.01 per cent per annum of interest x the face value of the contract (500,000) x one quarter of a year = £12.50.

Being worried that the interest rate will rise the borrower sells one June contract at 90.00. By 31 May, when the borrowing is rolled over, the interest rate has risen to 12 per cent. The result of the hedge is shown below.

Money Market	**Futures market**
1 February	Sells one June contract
Fears rise in rates by rollover	at 90.00 (rate = 10 per cent)
31 May	Buys back futures at 88.00
Rolls over at 12 per cent	(rate = 12 per cent)
Extra cost	Gain
2 per cent on £0.5m for	200 ticks at £12.50
one quarter = £2,500	= £2,500

This hedge worked perfectly – the gain on futures was exactly equal to the extra interest, and achieved a net borrowing cost of 10 per cent per annum. In practice such perfect matching is rare. Futures prices may not move exactly in line with cash market rates. If interest rates had fallen, the hedger's loss on his futures position would have been matched by lower interest payments, so that his net borrowing cost would still have been 10 per cent per annum.

5
Methods of Measuring Corporate Solvency

Examples of Credit Assessment

Rotaprint plc failed in February 1988 with a loss to the creditors of over £3m. This was a public corporation requiring full disclosure of accounting, press and statutory data. The abbreviated accounts, set out in Fig 17, show declining sales over a four-year period and varying losses from 1985 onwards. During the period, net worth declined and bank debt increased. At the year-end, 29 March 1987, there was a funding issue applied to a reduction of both short- and long-term borrowings.

Rotaprint plc

Model : 1 - Quoted Industrial
Industry : 69 - Office Equipment

Date updated : 20.04.88
Latest Year end : 29.03.87

	29.03.87	29.03.86	30.03.85	31.03.84
Period ends	29.03.87	29.03.86	30.03.85	31.03.84
Months in period end	12	12	12	12

PROFIT AND LOSS ACCOUNT (£)

Sales	13786	14914	15541	15663
Profit before tax	-502	-989	-662	168
Depreciation	171	115	97	58
Interest charge	225	358	311	208
Deferred tax charge	0	0	0	0
Minority interest	0	0	0	0
Retained profit	-502	-965	-696	94

METHODS OF MEASURING CORPORATE SOLVENCY

ASSETS EMPLOYED

Fixed assets at NBV	608	928	1002	214
Intangible assets	0	0	0	0
Other assets (assoc co)	0	0	0	0

CURRENT ASSETS

Stock	4101	3932	4494	5138
Debtors	2907	2873	3242	3152
Other current assets	14	24	0	0
TOTAL CURRENT ASSETS	7058	6859	7791	8358

CURRENT LIABILITIES

Creditors	3068	3448	3195	3501
Debut due within 2 years	1450	2295	2029	1453
Other liabilities	0	0	0	0
TOTAL CURRENT LIABILITIES	4518	5743	5224	4959

WORKING CAPITAL	2540	1116	2567	3399

NET CAPITAL EMPLOYED	3148	2044	3569	3613

FINANCED BY

TOTAL NET WORTH	2779	1523	2828	3030
Debt repayable after 2 yrs	0	0	0	0
Unanalysed loans 2-5 yrs	369	521	741	0
Provisions	0	0	0	0

TOTAL FUNDS EMPLOYED	3148	2044	3569	3613

RATIO ANALYSIS

Profit Margin (%)	-3.64	-6.63	-4.26	1.07
Return on Net Worth (%)	-18.06	-64.94	-23.41	5.54
Debt Equity Ratio (%)	64.16	182.93	96.00	64.95
Current Ratio	1.57	1.20	1.50	1.69
Acid Test Ratio	0.65	0.51	0.63	0.64
Days Debtors	76.97	70.31	76.14	73.45
Days Creditors	81.23	84.39	75.04	81.58
Stock Turn	3.36	3.79	3.46	3.05
Fixed Asset T/O	22.67	16.07	15.51	73.19
Return on Assets (%)	-3.63	-8.13	-4.02	4.42

Fig. 17   Abbreviated accounts for Rotaprint plc

Credit controllers might have been warned of this failure by reference to three different approaches represented by Dun & Bradstreet, Credit Ratings and Syspas.

The Approach of Dun & Bradstreet Ltd

Dun & Bradstreet (D & B) is a very well established US-based international corporation with wide interests in information–based systems. From a background of credit information, the company has a leading position in marketing and market research, publishing and investor services such as Moody's. It operates in many countries of the free world.

In Britain, D & B has two prime sources of information which it uses flexibly to provide customers with both financial and payment data. Firstly, the filed accounts of over 800,000 companies are analysed relative to their industrial

---

Payment Analysis Report

Rotaprint plc	PAYMENT SCORE 65
Rotaprint House,	** Key **
Honeypot Lane,	SCORE PAYMENT
LONDON NW9 9RE UK	100 Anticipate
	90 Discount
	80 Prompt
	70 Slow to 15
	50 Slow to 30
	40 Slow to 60
	30 Slow to 90
	20 Slow to 120
	UN Unavailable

Chief Executive Michael B. Manzi, FCCA, ACMA

Any Amounts Hereafter Are in Local Currency Unless Otherwise Stated

Started 1927 Sales 13,786,000

SIC 3555 3579 Litho Print and Duplicating Machine Manufacturers

The Industry Quartiles are taken from the ICC Database's Industrial Statistics on: printing, bookbinding and paper goods machinery.

Fig. 18   Dun & Bradstreet's sample payment score

sector. The second is the payment score, gleaned from a monthly examination of the sales ledger tapes of 2,000 major companies. D & B estimate that the analysis covers over 80 per cent of the businesses on their database; the remaining 20 per cent of information is derived from a written request to individual companies, seeking customer payment experience. A sample payment score is shown in Fig. 18 which sets out the overall rating of the company.

D & B has global files on 16 million companies of which 7 million are in the USA and 5.4 million in Europe. The reporting format differs in each country due to the disclosure requirements; however, most reports include data provided by individual concerns such as type of business, size of company, sales, net worth, directors and major shareholders. Most companies will be given a payment score based on the analysis of sales ledgers.

A further innovation is the D & B Alert Service culled twice weekly from the *London Gazette* and *Stubbs Directory* (a D & B service compiled from the Cardiff and Edinburgh Company Registration Offices' magnetic tapes). Depending upon the level of information required, clients are alerted to significant changes in the payment, financial or legal status of their customers.

D&B in Relation to Rotaprint

Subscribers would have received an abbreviated set of accounts and a ratio analysis similar to that shown in Fig 17. In addition, the payment score in Fig 18 would have given the credit controller the view that the company had a 'median' payment record. Finally, subscribers to the Alert Service would have been informed that the directors had sought funds from the company's pension scheme in the latter half of 1987.

The Approach of Credit Ratings Ltd

The company is a subsidiary of ICC Ltd, a London-based company that provides an information service either on-line or indirectly of over 90,000 British and Irish companies. ICC can also supply data from 3,500 Canadian businesses and has links with equivalent European and US firms supplying financial and stock-dealing data. Although ICC is primarily a provider of credit information, the large database is also available for market research and company comparisons (within the SIC industrial codes). Reports are available on market sectors and ICC can provide mailings to shareholders holding more than 0.25 per cent of British listed and USM companies.

ICC Credit Rating
The ICC credit score is an empirical rating of 1 to 100 based on ratios weighting the company in relation to its industrial sector. A score of less than 30 implies that a company is at risk of failure. About 50 per cent of the credit score is profit related; the remaining 50 per cent concerns the stock turnover (10 per cent), credit period (10 per cent), liquidity ratio (10 per cent) and current ratio (20 per cent).

Financial Summary and Credit Opinion
ICC produces a ratio analysis related to its industrial sector on the same page as a financial summary and credit opinion. Each company is analysed, the credit score reported and the reader is provided with a proposed credit limit. The sample sheet for Rotaprint is shown in Fig 19

ICC in Relation to Rotaprint
The credit score of 26 in Fig 19 places the company below the risk level of 30. The main cause for concern is the low level of profitability (also identified by D & B); however, subscribers might have been comforted by the reduced borrowing ratios and financial summary comment.

The Approach of Syspas Ltd

The company was started in 1979 to develop the work of Professor Richard Taffler's doctoral thesis on solvency prediction using the Z-Score. The Z-Score was originally applied to financial analysis in the USA by Professor Eward Altman of New York University. He used a technique known as

ROTAPRINT PLC
RATIO ANALYSIS

		Company Results		Industry Quartiles		
		Later	Earlier	Lower	Median	Upper
Current ratio	ratio	1.6	1.2	1.0	1.2	1.7
Liquidity ratio	ratio	0.7	0.5	0.6	0.8	1.1
Profit margin	%	-3.4	-8.6	0.0	2.8	8.0
Profitability	%	-6.2	-16.6	0.1	4.2	10.2
Stock turnover	ratio	3.4	3.8	4.0	5.9	9.2
Credit period	days	73.9	69.0	80.6	62.9	43.8
Borrowing ratio	%	65.5	201.3	103.2	46.3	12.5
Debt equity		13.3	34.2	30.1	6.9	0.0
Work Cap/Sales	%	18.4	7.5	16.7	8.8	1.1

Financial Summary and Credit Opinion

Credit Score × 26. The group has a poor credit score and considerable caution is needed in reaching a credit decision.

Calculated upper limit for trade credit × £140,000.

Turnover has fallen by 7.5 per cent during the year, however a 13 per cent drop in the direct cost of sales has led to an increase in gross profits. Nevertheless, distribution and administrative costs remain high and the group has incurred a loss for the third consecutive year. The resultant profit margin and profitability ratios, whilst improving as a result of the smaller loss for the year, still compare poorly even with a sector in which one quarter of companies also incurred losses during the year.

There has been a slight improvement in the current and liquidity ratios over the year (principally as a result of the drop in the bank overdraft from £1,835,000 in 1986 to £1,239,000 in 1987) but whilst the former is now satisfactory in both absolute and relative terms, the high level of stocks (hence the low stock turnover) means that the latter remains weak.

The longer-term position of the group has been heavily influenced by a combination of share capital changes and movements in the capital and revaluation reserves. This has left the group with an improved level of shareholders' funds now representing 36 per cent (1986 = 20 per cent) of the group's total assets. This indicates a moderate long-term financial position although it is important to note that speculation in the group's shares after Big Bang artificially boosted the share price without any 'underlying reason' and such volatility cannot be conducive to stable outlook for the company.

Fig. 19   Credit Rating Ltd's Rating Report

multiple discriminant analysis to analyse and weigh the most significant ratios that distinguish between previous failed and healthy companies. When a company had a Z-Score below a defined threshold it was at risk of failure.

Taffler extended Altman's work in two significant ways. Firstly, he ranked a company's Z-Score with others to derive a percentile or PAS-Score for plotting on a graph. Secondly, he further developed the ratio analysis to highlight the strengths and weaknesses, so directing the analyst to the relevant areas in the original accounts. Syspas holds data for the 3,500 larger UK listed and unlisted companies and this is provided to subscribers on disks to be worked on personal computers with software licensed by Syspas.

Syspas in Relation to Rotaprint

The graphical and ratio analysis described above is shown for Rotaprint in Fig 20 and Chart 9 (overleaf), which illustrate the principles of the Syspas technique.

Rotaprint Plc

Model : 1 - Quoted Industrial
Industry : 69 - Office Equipment

PAS Year	Prof Marg*	Work Cap*	Fin Risk*	Liqui-dity*	PAS Score**	Z-Score***	Ind****
1981	--	4	1	2	3	-4.79	50
1982	4	8	3	5	40	1.99	44
1983	2	7	2	3	20	0.13	40
1984	--	7	1	3	6	-2.98	36
1985	--	4	1	2	1	-5.59	34
1986	1	7	1	3	8	-2.02	28

Risk Rating: 2

Latest Year End: 29.03.87

Fig. 20   The Syspas Technique
*   score out of 10 (10 v.good, -- v.poor)
**   score out of 100 (100 v.good, 1 v.poor)
***   a - (minus) sign shows company at risk
****   average PAS score for office equipment

METHODS OF MEASURING CORPORATE SOLVENCY

1   The trajectory graph shows the company to have been at risk since 1983; after falling to a low in 1985, it staged a revival due to the rights issue. At the time of failure the graph showed the company was at risk – it being below the solvency threshold.

2   The main reason for the failure was the weakness in profitability and the large financial risk of the third ratio.

3   The risk rating of 2 shows the company to have a 43 per cent risk of failure in the next financial year. It should be noted that in 1985 the risk rating before the rights issue was 5, indicating 90 per cent chance of failure (at the very least).

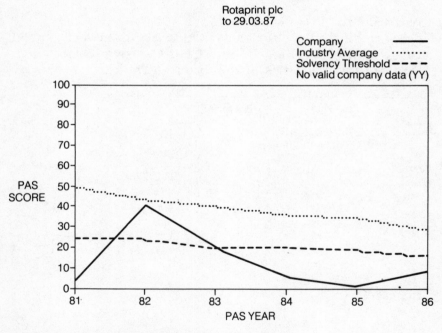

Chart 9   The Syspas Technique trajectory graph

154

Sequence of Events During the Twenties and Thirties and Comparison With the Present

Comparisons Between Events in the United States, the United Kingdom, Germany and Other Countries

A THE PLATEAU PHASE (*continued overleaf*)

UNITED STATES
1920–5

- Warren Harding President until 1923: replaced by VP Calvin Coolidge.
- Wartime expansion created inflation.
- Federal rate increased from 4 to 7 per cent (M1 fell 9%).
- Wholesale prices down 40% in one year; US$ backed by over $0.34 in gold. US owned 28% gold stocks.
- New building increased 400% after Federal Reserve Bank eased credit.
- European deposits in USA increased to $150bn (1986$) – $ overvalued.
- Monetary ease. Yield on thirty-year bond declined from c 5½% to 3¾%.
- Start of stock market speculation; economy boomed.
- Unemployment 2–5% through period.
- Massive lending to Europe following Weimar inflation.
- Foodstuff overproduction – 48% of US exports.
- US tariffs on dutiable goods at c 40%.

UNITED KINGDOM
1920–5

- Lloyd George PM until 1922, then Bonar Law. Minority Labour Government 1924.
- Cunliffe Committee recommended return to gold standard. Enacted at $4.86/£1 in April 1925. Bank Rate raised to 5%.
- Geneva Convention in 1922 allowed bonds and bills as bank reserves with gold.
- Unemployment 18%. Coal, textiles and steel hardest hit.
- Up to 85% of all tariffs duty free.

GERMANY and others
1920–5

- Wartime export restrictions encouraged developing countries to set up coal, textile and ferrous industries.
- Germany: Weimar republic massive war reparation at up to £125m/year.
- 1923: Dr Schacht introduced 'Rentenmark' secured on land and industry to stop runaway inflation that valued Reichsmark at 18,000m to the £ sterling. Inflation wiped out all savings and eliminated German creditors. This paved the way for the Nazis who fought elections and gained control in 1933. See 'Depression Phase' below.

UNITED STATES
1926–8

- 1928. Herbert Hoover elected President.
- Farmers' representatives dominate Senate, terms of trade decline.
- Yield curve negative 1927.
- Federal budget surplus.

UNITED KINGDOM
1926–8

- Baldwin PM until 1928 when MacDonald elected as minority PM.
- 1926 General Strike in support of miners. Wages cut.
- Budget deficit.
- Staple industries in decline.

GERMANY and others
1926–8

- German expansion based on foreign credits and loans. US credits up to $5bn.
- Developing countries' incomes declined due to reduced commodity prices.

B THE CRISIS PHASE

UNITED STATES
1929

- Bank lending on margin for stock exchange speculation, funds withdrawn from Europe.
- Commodity prices declined.
- Aug. production declined, Federal Reserve Bank tightened credit to reduce speculation.
- Sept. Dow peaked.
- Oct. Wall Street Crash; Dow Jones down 50% by Dec (regained over 50%, spring 1930).
- New building down 30% since 1925.
- Federal budget surplus.
- Datum of 100 for GNP, M1.

UNITED KINGDOM
1929

- Clarence Hatry steel group failed.
- Low tariffs attracted imports.
- Budget deficit.
- Datum of 100 for GNP, M1.

GERMANY and others
1929

- US banks reduced deposits in German and Austrian banks.
- Financing 37% from USA; 20% from UK.
- Datum of 100 for German GNP, M1.

UNITED STATES
1930

- Hoover signed Hawley-Smoot Act in June. Farm tariffs increased. Democrats won House of Representatives.
- Farming contraction, bankruptcies and rural bank failures.
- Increased withdrawal of funds from Europe.
- Federal budget and current account surplus.
- GNP 91; M1 97.

UNITED KINGDOM
1930

- Bank rate 5%.
- Increasing budget deficit.
- Trade deficit.

GERMANY and others
1930

- Credit Anstalt loss Sept, first run on Reichsbank followed withdrawal of US deposits.
- Defensive tariffs to Hawley-Smoot.
- German Prod Index 86; M1 97.

1931 — United States

- Sept/Oct: rush to buy gold; reserves down by $725m. NY.
- Reserve Bank increases discount rate from 2.5% to 3.5%.
- Aug 1931–Jan 1932: 1,860 banks fail with deposits of $1.5bn.
- Long bond starts rapid fall.
- Unemployment 16.3%.
- RFC provides Federal credit to banks; enacted by Hoover.
- GNP 86; M1 91.

UNITED STATES
1932

- RFC passed funds to save Central Bank, Chicago.
- Long bond touched 66.
- April: rush on gold.
- Property foreclosures, values down 80% from peak (see HOLC below).
- Roosevelt elected President.
- Unemployment 24.1%.
- GNP 73; M1 79.

1933 to 1940

- March: FDR took office. Bank crisis. FDR ordered holiday. Gold exports stopped and $US devalued to $35.02; $ depreciation 40%.
- 40% of all banks had failed; peak of business failures.
- Monetary expansion, cheap credit, confiscation of gold and gold instruments.
- *First New Deal – 100 days.*

1931 — United Kingdom

- July/Aug: overseas loans frozen and funds withdrawn from Britain.
- Pound defended in Aug but not Sept.
- 10 Sept: Govt supplementary budget, expenditures cut.
- Home Fleet mutinies.
- 16 Sept: run on sterling.
- 21 Sept: Britain off gold standard, pound devalued by 25%.
- 21 Oct: National Govt formed.
- GNP 95; M1 91.

C THE DEPRESSION PHASE

UNITED KINGDOM
1932

- Ottawa Conference introduced Imperial Preference with UK.
- Exchange equalisation a/c buffered credit markets from 'hot money'.
- Unemployment peaked at 23%.
- GNP 96; M1 108.

1933 to 1940

- UK budget balanced, small current a/c deficit.
- Tariffs 37% no duty
  33% – 10%
  15% – 11–20%
  5% – 72%
- Increase of bilateral trading and quota system.
- Increase in cartels and monopolies.

1931 — Germany

- March: further run on Reichsbank. Hoover proposes moratorium.
- North German Wool Co fails. Danat Bank fails.
- June: war reparations suspended.
- Aug: interest payments suspended
- Other countries off gold standard.
- Competitive devaluations.
- Peru and Chile suspend debt payments.
- German Prod Ind 68; M1 94.

GERMANY and others
1932

- Mexico suspends payments for three years.

1933 to 1940

- Jan 33: Hitler appointed Chancellor – planned economy and controls.
- Nazis introduced closed economy and drastically increased public expenditure.
- Employment created in public works, bureaucracy, compulsory labour and armed forces. Inflation controlled by tax increases and direction of income into investment from consumer items.

UNITED STATES

- AAA passed to support farm prices and reduce output.
- FERA relief grant to States.
- CURA first attempt at public works – terminated 1934.
- CCC formed to plant forests, etc.
- TVA in Tennessee Valley.
- NRA introduced national planning. Also sought to regulate minimum wages and maximum working hours. Increased union and large company power. Declared unconstitutional in 1935.
- HOLC refinance at low interest: up to 20% of private homes.
- SEC regulated Stock Exchange. SE lost 85% from peak.
- Unemployment peaked at 25.2%.
- 1933: GNP 71; M1 75
- *Second New Deal* in 1936.
- WPA started with $1.48m in 1934, combination of arts and manual work projects. Increased in 1935.
- By 1940: gold flowing into US at $3.5bn/year.
- Gold reserves 60% of world and yield on bonds down to 2½%.
- In US Govt measures took leftward political stance.

UNITED KINGDOM

- State organisations formed, eg BBC, BOAC, CEGB, Forestry Commission.
- Little legislation. Aim to balance budget and maintain interior rates at 2%.
- Boom in property in South and Midlands and construction employment increased.
- New industries, motors, radios, domestic appliances, electrical engineering. Increase in investment and employment.
- Decline in staple textiles, mining, steel and shipping.
- Agriculture manning decline, increased mechanisation.
- Increase in distribution efficiency.
- Shift from rail to motor transport.
- Utilities increased, more homes electrified.
- Volume of production up 20% from 1929 to 1939.
- Coalition Government, centre right. MacDonald premier until 1935 when Baldwin elected as Conservative leader.

GERMANY and others

- External trade organised to buy raw materials, substitute imports and conclude political trading deals.
- Export surplus through export subsidies, exchange controls and 'clearing system'.
- In Europe politics moved to the right with Fascism in Germany, Italy, Spain and – latterly – France.
- Sept 33: Brazil declared 'temporary' moratorium bond conversion. Unilateral suspension, 1937.

7

The Principles of Franchising

The problem of high new business failure is largely over-come in franchising because of the way the business format is formulated, tested and proven. The franchisee is provided with the systems for training, marketing and start-up in exchange for a franchise fee. Management service fees are earned (generally as a royalty) for providing support ser-vices during the life of the contract.

The relationship between a franchisor and franchisee is incorporated in the form of a licence agreement, outline details of which are:

- The franchisor has the name, idea, process, business method or specialised piece of equipment that is licensed to the franchisee.
- The agreement obliges the franchisor to provide the franchisee with a blueprint for starting up and staying in business through training, the provision of manuals and follow-up support.
- The franchisee owns his business, provides the funds and is responsible for management and recruitment. The concern is run according to the standards set out in the licence agreement and operations manual.
- Payment for granting the franchise is usually a down pay-ment for the business format and a management service fee for continued support.
- The agreement includes a termination date and option to renegotiate the agreement.

8

The Advantages of Franchising

The benefits of franchising have been successfully tested in the developed world and particularly in the USA where around five million people are employed in service or retail activities. The business format method enables the franchisor to create and control dedicated independent outlets with the minimum expenditure of fixed and working capital.

The advantages to both the franchisor and franchisee are:

For the Franchisor
- An income stream is often created for a parent company from what otherwise would be a marginal activity because the process cuts off layers of management and expense. For the smaller company, revenue is available without extending management or financial resources.
- The business format process enables the franchisor to control and maintain the products or services sold. Each of the outlets is committed to running its own business according to the franchisor's business formula.
- Franchising in many cases allows the franchisor to standardise manufacturing or distribution operations, because the finishing process may be completed by the franchisee. At the same time expansion is created without the need for additional working or fixed capital.

For the Franchisee
- Individuals are provided with the opportunity to own and manage their own business.
- The business is tested and proven. This reduces failure rates for franchisees to less than 4 per cent compared to normal start-up experience of over 20 per cent.
- Training in business is provided with continuing advice and support.

THE ADVANTAGES OF FRANCHISING

- Trading is conducted under a distinctive brand name, process or skill.
- A capital investment is created.
- Outside funds are obtainable as business grows.
- Business start-up is accelerated.

9

Case Study: Industrial Services Company (ISC)

Impact of Franchising the Branch Operations of ISC

INDUSTRIAL SERVICES COMPANY (ISC)

Impact of Phoenix Asset Recovery Programme on the Operating Statement

Revenue position at 31.12.85   £000s

	Branches owned by ISL		Branches franchised	
Sales		6,700	Ref 1	7,380
Income		6,700	Ref 2	738
Costs	6,100		Ref 3	360
Depreciation	370		Ref 4	75
Administration	30		Ref 3	30
Interest payable	140		Ref 5	(20)
Profit before tax		60		293
Persons employed		290	Ref 6	10

Reference 1: Franchising existing operations almost invariably lifts sales by over 20 per cent due to the added commitment of the franchisees. A conservative 10 per cent has been allowed. No additional revenue has been allowed for creating additional franchisees at minimum additional cost to the franchisor – see Chapter 13.

Reference 2: The income from a franchise consists of royalties from the franchisees. The reduced operating costs of the branches allows 10 per cent to be paid to ISC.

Reference 3: Franchising transfers the direct costs of running a branch to the franchisee, leaving the franchisor with only the minimum administration.

Reference 4: Ownership of fixed assets (including vehicles) by the franchisee reduces depreciation by around 80 per cent.

Reference 5: The interest payable is converted to a notional interest receivable from the loan to the parent.

Reference 6: It is a feature of franchising that the output per person is radically improved because the franchising staff can mainly concentrate on development, marketing and servicing franchisees. Throughout this programme, it is assumed that the branches will be transferred into separate companies before being formed into franchises; this will achieve the greatest flexibility for the franchisor and will avoid liability for redundancy payments.

CASE STUDY: INDUSTRIAL SERVICES COMPANY (ISC)

INDUSTRIAL SERVICES COMPANY (ISC)

Impact of Phoenix Asset Recovery Programme on the Balance Sheet

Balance sheet at 31.12.85, £000s

	Branches owned			Branches franchised
Fixed assets	1,500	Ref 1		300
Stocks	48	Ref 2	48	
Debtors	1,800	Ref 3	200	
Cash	10		10	
	1,858		258	
Less				
Creditors	330	Ref 4	60	
Loan	1,650	Ref 5	-	
Taxation	110		110	
Accruals	170	Ref 6	-	
Finance	140	Ref 6	-	
	(542)			88
Finance leases	(40)	Ref 6		-
Deferred tax	(380)	Ref 1	(76)	
Parent loan	-	Ref 5		226
Net assets	538			538

Reference 1: 80 per cent of fixed assets sold to the franchisees at net book value and equivalent deferred tax paid to the revenue.

Reference 2: Inventory held by franchisor to service franchisees.

Reference 3: Debtors pro-rata with income.

Reference 4: Creditors mainly confined to financing inventory.

Reference 5: The net cash position of £226,000 is derived from the sale of assets less payment of creditors (see other references). Part of the asset sales are applied to paying off the parent loan.

Reference 6: Finance charges and accruals paid off when assets transferred to franchisees.

10
Case History:
Plant Hire Company (PHC)

PHC is one of the largest plant-hire businesses in Europe, it operates and maintains many thousand items of equipment from twenty-two depots in Britain. Recently, a new service has been initiated for maintaining customer's own plant at their premises. The board of PHC see franchising as an opportunity to expand their strength of engineers without increasing their cost base and the Centre of Franchise Marketing (CFM) was asked to undertake a study. The aim was to:

- Expand PHC's present position in the market-place with increased engineering strength.
- Maximise the utilisation of PHC depot administrative and technical expertise.
- Obtain a significant cash-flow stream at all levels.

In addition, it was hoped that franchising would:

- Increase customer contact leading to additional contract hire business.
- Increase the sales of spares and other services.

The franchising feasibility report identified the following benefits to PHC:

- To increase engineer strength at a far lower investment cost than hiring more staff and acquiring more vehicles.
- To increase market penetration and customer attention.
- To increase market presence with more vehicles on the road displaying the PHC logo.
- To introduce a new form of worker commitment.

- To offer an earnings package which would attract the 'pick of the crop' of the best plant engineers available in the UK.
- To maximise management motivational strengths of the depot.
- To obtain the benefit of fixed pricing together with increase production – resulting in increased revenue.
- In marketing terms the market research undertaken and included in the report highlighted the urgent need for PHC to increase its 'local' presence to counter strong competitive activity.

The Financial Benefits

It was envisaged that by the end of the third year of the franchising plan PHC would have between sixty-six and seventy-two franchisees making a combined contribution to PHC head office and depot amounting to between £400,000 and £674,000. However, prior to embarking on a full-scale franchising plan it was recommended that pilot tests be undertaken. It was envisaged that the cost of the tests would be of the order of £50,000 which would be offset by income of some £17,000.

Implications for PHC

The success of franchising in the UK today is initially due in no small measure to the entrepreneurial drive of the franchisor. To achieve this, it was essential, right from the start, for PHC to appoint a franchise champion to provide the 'drive' to get the franchise off the ground. It was evident that in the following years the management strength of PHC could well prove to be the making of a first-class franchise organisation.

A further study showed the benefits to PHC if their existing engineers became franchisees. Principally there were five areas of cost reduction:

- Capital costs.   The cost of putting a man and a vehicle on the road.

- Working capital. The cost of funding his sales revenue. If he is supplying a service to industry on an account basis the length of payment often averages around two months.
- The engineer's direct operating costs. The actual direct operating cost of the engineer himself such as his vehicle running costs, insurance, wages and holiday pay, etc.
- Field management and head-office costs. The management and administration costs of running directly employed engineers.
- Interest and depreciation. Interest on funding debtors and depreciation on vehicles and equipment.

An indication of the typical savings that can be enjoyed are given below:

- Capital costs. Fully fitted out vehicle, spares stock, equipment, tools: £12,000
- Working capital. If the engineer achieves a turnover of £48,000 in a year, two months' debtors on average: £8,000
- Engineer's direct costs. Vehicle running costs, insurance, telephones, wages, holiday pay, etc. £16,000
- Management costs and head-office costs: As much as one-third
- Interest and depreciation. Interest on the capital cost of the vehicle and equipment and working capital at say 16 per cent plus. Depreciation on the vehicle and equipment over four years on a straightline basis: £6,200

Note When converting present employees to become franchisees redundancy must be agreed and paid before the new relationship can begin.

11

The Rank Xerox Experience

The photocopier patents of Rank Xerox (RX) ran out in 1979. The machines were electro-mechanical in operation and were vulnerable to new electronic designs produced mainly by Canon of Japan. The electronic products considerably undercut existing copiers and RX were faced with major problems of redesign and under-recovery of overheads.

The company responded to the acute competitive position through the classical procedures described in Chapter 3 implying factory and head-office rationalisation. There was also expansion at the electronics plant in Hertfordshire as new designs were launched. The new factor in the cost reduction programme was a fresh look at the value of staff overheads.

The problem facing RX was to devise a method of retaining the skills of certain key individuals while, if possible, reducing their cost of employment. Taking everything into account, this was estimated to be over three times their salary working from a London office. The solution devised by a team working under Philip Judkins was to seek volunteers who would still work for RX but be based at home. The plan was for the individuals to form their own companies and work under contract for the parent but be free to seek non-competing work elsewhere.

The first volunteer for the pilot scheme was one of their personnel managers, Roger Walker, who set up his own company, Chamberlains Personnel Services Ltd at Stony Stratford near Milton Keynes. The plan was for Walker to evaluate the psychological, economic and administrative problems of working for himself and then report back. The report, compiled over a twelve-month period, involved both feedback from the field and essential contributions from staff at all levels. The results were positive and Walker's experience was incorporated into a second pilot test. Eventually some sixty executives became independent.

The implications and results were remarkable:

- In addition to redundancy payments RX had guaranteed each individual 50 per cent of their previous salary for the first year to be contracted on a job basis. The individuals appeared on the organisation chart of the company, attended meetings etc, their time being invoiced at an agreed rate.
- There was an increase of individual productivity of about 100 per cent only partly due to the incentive of being self-employed (the franchising experience is at least 20 per cent). The new relationship forced the company into defining tasks with greater precision and detachment from head office enabled work to be carried out with less disturbance. A further, and unforeseen, bonus was the added career prospect for secretaries who were the main link in the communication between the company and their newly independent bosses.
- The cost saving to RX was over £2.5m. This was made up by the estimated saving of one and a half times the salaries of sixty people earning an average of £30,000.
- An important feature of the programme was the intercommunication set up to link RX with remote workers. Each person had a computer that was connected through a modem and Telecom line to the head-office computer for receiving and transmitting messages and work. In practice this benefitted some skills more than others, but the system was considered a valuable asset and has now taken a more permanent form in the Xanadu Association based at High Wycombe. Ex-RX employees can communicate their services and keep in touch with others through a network organised by the association.

Note on Communication through Electronic Mail

Electronic mail (E-Mail) is a method whereby messages can be transmitted and received through a computer network. Although individual computers can be linked together, the

THE RANK XEROX EXPERIENCE

system generally requires a host mainframe linked to outstations through Telecom lines.

E-Mail networks may be either private or public depending upon the size of the organisation and may link customers and suppliers as well as employees. For example, ICI networks one hundred sales managers and some seven hundred salesmen from its own mainframe; smaller businesses might use a public system such as Telecom Gold. A public system provides subscribers with an electronic pigeon hole through which messages can be left and retrieved.

12

The Experience of F International and CPS

F International (FI) and Contract Programming Service (CPS) are two companies that make extensive use of remote workers and provide their customers with computer programming and related services. Both can serve as a working model for companies wishing to reduce fixed costs through Grade 2 remote working (see Chapter 14).

F International Group plc is a most unusual company started by Mrs Steve Shirley to mobilise the professional programming skills of women many of whom had left full-time employment for family reasons. The aim, according to the company's charter, was 'to develop, through modern telecommunications, the unutilised intellectual energy of individuals and groups unable to work in a conventional environment'.

The company achieved sales of around £10m in 1987 and employs about a thousand people, over 75 per cent of whom work from their homes. The 'panel', as the remote workers are called, undertake to work for an agreed minimum time per week, either at regional offices or on clients' premises. The task that F International has mastered is to mobilise the panel's skills in the most efficient manner:

- From the headquarters at Berkhamsted, Hertfordshire, the company employs the central administration including finance, marketing, technical development and the divisional directors.
- The divisional directors control regional managers, who work from five offices around Britain; it is the managers' task to organise the home-based panel of around 750 people. The majority of people who are responsible for supervising clients' work are salaried.

- Members of the panel have an average of four years' professional experience and work from the regional offices or on clients' premises. The tasks include programming, systems analysis, lecturing, project management, training and estimating.
- The panel members are self-employed for tax purposes and for this reason must be demonstrably independent. Members are paid by the hour depending upon their skill and responsibility (the rate discounts the free-market fees for their equivalent skills by the costs of marketing, management etc).
- FI has developed the particular management skills needed to match the spirit and responsibilities of the panel with the contractual responsibility to the client. The company acknowledges that this method of working requires higher management ratios than would be needed in a more conventional environment.

Contract Programming Service (CPS) is a subsidiary of ICL that was first started as a field support unit to launch the 2900 Series of mainframe computers. The origins are similar to F International in that remote working was considered a sensible method of retaining the professional skills of women who would otherwise have retired to raise a family. Although all work initially originated from the parent company, CPS now tenders increasingly outside ICL.

Unlike F International, the 180 remote workers are employees who receive a pension and a minimum retainer of sixteen hours per week. CPS draws upon ICL for a number of group services but needs a similar approach to FI for managing their employees in the field.

13
Agency Working in the USA

Agency sales are growing rapidly in the US. This is because they provide an experienced and relatively low cost entry into sales territories that would be costly to penetrate through direct selling. Agencies work on commission which is a variable cost to the principal.

One calculation showed that for similar costs, agencies multiplied a manufacturer's field strength by around six times compared with the fixed expense of direct representation. Agencies act for several non-competing principals and new management skills are needed to get the best out of the relationship.

This appendix describes agency working in the USA and the requirements for a successful relationship. There are four sections:

- Sales agencies in the USA.
- Agency formation.
- Pros and cons of agency working.
- Agency agreements.

Sales Agencies in the USA

Working with agents is a common fact of life for generating overseas business. It is less common for agencies to be used for internal selling as they are in the USA. Some features are:

- Scale of agency working. It is estimated that there are around 30,000 sales agencies in the USA employing 105,000 individuals.
- Average agencies generate around $4m gross sales annually for their principals from three highly qualified salespersons covering five states.
- Product coverage is considerable, ranging from hi-tech

172

electronics through to toys. One of the largest agency associations, Manufacturers' Agents National Association (MANA), covers over ninety industries.

- Agency usage is extensive. A survey by the Research Institute of America Inc (RIA) showed that on average about 50 per cent of all manufacturers used agencies; this rises to over 80 per cent in electrical machinery and equipment. Agencies are used also for sales through distributors.

- Agency coverage is widespread and there are few places in the US not served. An analysis of Electronic Representatives Association (ERA) members shows a considerable choice of representation. The average-sized agency employs around five persons. In most areas there is a range between the small specialist of one or two persons up to a business employing as many as fifty.

- Choice of agency will be affected by the impact of a new line on the 'portfolio' of products carried. Normally technical agencies will not be able to do justice to more than ten lines, and any new product should contribute over 5 per cent of the new level of sales.

- Agency support by the principal is essential for both parties to achieve the most from the relationship. Agents will also expect a rapid response to quotation requests and customer complaints.

- Commissions payable vary from 1 to 40 per cent with a concentration between 5 and 8 per cent. The commission increases with the skills and experience of people in the agency and some manufacturers are prepared to give more commission in exchange for a higher agency commitment.

Agency Formation

Agency working has been a feature of most industrialised countries and the USA, in particular, because of its size. Almost all have been started by ex-direct salesmen who decided that they could make a better living on their own, despite a high failure record. Originally agencies tended to be non-specialised and carried a range of products in the hope that their regular accounts would take at least something from their catalogue.

173

The emphasis changed with the advent of specialised electronic and hi-tech products which considerably increased the skill level. Agents were still recruited from ex-direct salesmen, in many cases with the encouragement of the parent company to avoid losing their abilities. Newly independent operators needed support and agency associations such as MANA in Laguna Hills, California and ERA in Chicago were formed.

Pros and Cons of Agency Working

Agencies now form an important part of representation in the USA, and their use should be compared with direct selling:

- A direct representative is estimated to cost at least $50,000 pa if locally based and up to $100,000 if much away travel is involved. On factory margins of 25 per cent, sales of over $200,000 to $400,000 will need to be generated before the territory breaks even. Agency commissions are a variable cost.
- Foreign manufacturers seeking representation will be attracted by the range of agency skills, the low cost of entry and sales coverage.
- The proliferation of agencies makes it possible for a manufacturer to mix direct and agency working. For example it may be decided to use direct selling for the most important house accounts and agencies for others.
- Where sales are made both to original equipment manufacturers (OEMs) and through distributors, the sales effort may be divided between direct selling for one and agency selling for the other.
- Agencies work exclusively on commission and it may be difficult to arouse their enthusiasm for some products that are either slow-moving or require pioneering.
- Agencies are more difficult to manage compared with direct control of salesmen. Sales managers need to learn new motivational and leadership skills dealing with representatives working for a different organisation.
- Historically, buyers have expressed a reluctance to deal

with agents. This is changing. Agents are becoming techni-cally better qualified and buyers appreciate that one call can cover a number of products.

Agency Agreements

The following paragraphs have been culled from the sample agreement between sales representatives and manufacturers as provided by the Electronics Representatives Association (ERA) of Chicago.

- The territory served by the agent can be defined in several different ways. For example, this may be in straight terri-torial terms or by type of customer. This may be further sub-divided in terms of distribution or OEM accounts. The agreement will also cover the products to be sold.
- The commission payable will vary depending upon service given, the pioneering work necessary, the reputation of the principal, etc. Agreements will specify any bonus pay-able, usually for exceeding pre-agreed targets.
- Commission is generally payable on the net invoice value to the customer less discounts, taxes, additional shipping charges, etc. The agent is entitled to receive copies of all invoices.
- The agent can only act on behalf of the principal and must follow the procedures laid down and agreed. There is generally no financial link between the agent and manu-facturer, although some bonus schemes allow for equity options.
- The agent is required to provide the necessary resource for successful representation. Manufacturers will supply the appropriate promotional material and be responsible for any required training of the agency representatives.
- Termination and the appropriate compensation must be included in the agreement. In general, compensation increases with the duration of the agency arrangement.

14

How the UK Milk Delivery Industry Converted Employees to Independence

A considerable proportion of milk consumed in Britain has traditionally been delivered to the door by roundsmen selling from vans supplied by retail depots. In the past, the depots were locally based dairies but the rise of national distributors has encouraged a considerable degree of concentration.

Within the last decade, the milk-round gallonage has been declining because of competition from supermarkets and increased female employment. To meet the threat the dairy nationals have considered ways of maintaining volume and reducing costs; one alternative has been franchising; this has reduced employment costs and arrested the decline in volume.

This appendix outlines the experience of the dairy industry in their form of franchising. Much of the material has been provided by Express Dairies. There are two sections:

- Franchising in the milk delivery industry.
- Pros and cons of independence.

Franchising in the Milk Delivery Industry

Franchising has a special application for the dairy industry; the franchisee does not have to make a high level of financial commitment and is still heavily dependent upon the parent depot:

- Franchisees are dependent upon wholesale milk supplies. If a depot closes milkmen have to travel further for supplies.

- Milkmen become self-employed after being made redundant and take over all the responsibilities of employee on-costs such as pension funding, social security payments, VAT and other accounting. Franchisees are also responsible for insuring the delivery van and anybody assisting on the round.
- Franchisees buy wholesale, collect debts from retail customers and settle weekly. The milkman receives a commission for non-retail sales made on behalf of the dairy.
- A franchise fee is charged by the franchisor for use of the depot facilities, use of the brand name and services provided by the franchisor. Milkmen are licensed to use the franchisor's name and benefit from any national promotion in their efforts to extend the gallonage delivered.
- Milk delivery vehicles are usually owned by the franchisor who leases the vans to the franchisees. Part of the franchise payment is made to house the vehicle and recharge the batteries (when the vehicles are electrically powered).
- Duration of the franchising contract is generally for one year with an agreed period of notice on either side. On termination, a positive goodwill payment is made if the gallonage has increased during the term of the contract, and a reverse charge if it has declined.

Pros and Cons of Independence

The dairy industry has found the prime benefit to lie in the added activity generated by independence and the reduced costs of employment:

- Franchising slows the decline in volume experienced by the industry.
- Franchisor expenses are reduced by the removal of employee pensions, holiday pay, social security etc but there would seem to be little impact on the administrative costs of the franchisor. The franchisee accepts the costs of dealing directly with the customer, for example, in wastage, debt collection etc.
- Labour turnover is reduced when rounds are franchised.
- Holiday and sickness cover is now the responsibility

177

of the franchisee. However, experience has shown that the depot management still needs to provide a stand-by resource.

- Round goodwill may pass over time to the franchisee which some franchisors perceive as loss of customers. This transfer is implicit in the licensing contract which franchisors need to keep current through product and promotion development.
- Management styles need to change when dealing with self-employed individuals. The franchisor will only benefit through increased wholesale volume and royalties if the franchisee is successful. This changes the role of previous managers into counsellors, encouragers and promoters. As much training needs to be given to the franchisor's management as to the franchisee.
- Personal problems have been experienced from individuals who, attracted to self-employment, find themselves unable to deal with the added administrative and personal responsibilities. In consequence, these burdens have fallen upon the depot managers, thus somewhat reducing the benefits of franchising.
- Labour unions oppose franchising on the grounds that the union member loses security in exchange for an increase of revenue. Opposition to franchising can cause problems for negotiation with mixed employee and franchised depots.

Further Reading

Aldcroft, D. H. *The British Economy Between the Wars* (Philip Allan)

Altman, Edward I. *Corporate Bankruptcy in America* (Heath Lexington Books)

Arndt, H. W. *The Economic Lessons of the 1930s* (Cass)

Batva, Ravi. *The Great Depression of 1990* (Venus)

Beckman, R. *Downwave* (Pan)

Blanchard, A. *How you Can Profit from the Panic of 1989*

Brinkley, A. Voices of Protest (Vintage)

Browning, I. and Garriss, E. *Past and Future History* (Fraser Publishing Company)

Congdon, T. *Debt Threat* (Blackwell)

Davidson, James and Rees-Mogg, Sir W. *Blood in the Streets* (Summit)

Economist, The. *Economic Statistics 1900–1983*

Erdman, P. *What's Next?* (Doubleday)

Ferguson, A. *When Money Dies* (William Kimber)

Galbraith, J. K. *The Great Crash, 1929* (Andre Deutsch)

Gann, W. D. *45 Years in Wall Street*

Hanzhang, General Tao. *Sun Tzu's Art of War* (David & Charles)

Hutchins, David. *Just in Time* (Gower Technical Press)

Judkins, P. West, D. and Drew J. *Networking within Organisations* (Gower Press)

Kindleberger, C. P. *Maniacs, Panics and Crashes* (Macmillan)

Kinsman, Francis. *The Telecommuters* (John Wiley & Sons)

Kirkland, W. and D. *Power Cycles* (Professional Communications)

Lever, H. and Huhne, C. *Debt and Danger* (Penguin)

McElvie, Robert S. *The Great Depression* (Times Books)

Morgan, Ted, FDR (Grafton)

Morris, M. *The General Strike* (Journeyman)

FURTHER READING

Naisbitt, John. *Megatrends* (Macdonald)

Pewett, G. *America in the Twenties* (Touchstone)

Saint-Etienne, C. *The Great Depression 1929–38, Lessons for the 1980s* (Hoover Institute)

Salinger, F. R. *Factoring and the Accountant in Practice* (Tooley)

Schultz, Harry. *Bear Markets* (Ted Morgan, FDR)

Slatter, Stuart. *Corporate Recovery* (Penguin)

Sprague, Irving I. *Bailout* (Basic Books Inc)

Stockman, D. *The Triumph of Politics* (Pan)

Thomas, H. *The Spanish Civil War* (Pelican)

Thomas, Morgan Witts. *The Day the Bubble Burst* (Penguin)

3is. *Buy-out, a Guide for Management* (3i)

Toffler, Alvin. *The Third Wave* (Pan Books)

Trost, A. J. and Prechter, R. *Elliott Wave Principle* (New Classics Library)

Weidlein, James and Cross, Thomas. *Networking Personal Computers in Organisations* (Kogan Page)

Acknowledgements

I would like to thank the following for their resource whilst I was writing this book.

British Venture Capital Association; 3i; Taylor Garrett; BCA Publications Ltd; Currencies and Credit Markets; Dow Theory Letters; Foster and Braithwaite Ltd; Investment Guideline Service; Naydale Services Ltd; World Money Analyst; Equipment Leasing Association and Finance Houses Association; BZW Futures Ltd; Investment Data Services Ltd; London International Financial Futures Exchange Ltd; Association of British Factors; Credit Ratings Ltd; Dun & Bradstreet Ltd; F. R. Salinger; Syspas Ltd; Trade Indemnity plc; Arthur Young Management Consultants; American Franchise Association; Centre for Franchise Marketing; Fixed Cost Reduction Ltd; Chamberlains Personnel Services Ltd; F International; Electronics Representatives Association; Manufacturers' Agents National Association; Bank Credit Analyst; Bridgewater Associates Inc; *The Economist*; *The Financial Times*; Hoare Govett Ltd; Sales Direction.
In particular I received help from the following individuals: Teddy Butler-Henderson; Richard Coghlan; John Cooper; Peter Crawley; Keith Dunlop; Mark Fletcher; Willem Foks; Richard Fox; David Galloway; John Gillum; Charles Hince; Janet Hipps; Denis Howson; Greg Hunt; Ian Jones; Michael Jordan; Philip Judkins; David Kimbell; Diana Norman; Michael Parish; Brian Pearse; Malcolm Reynell; David Sinker; Andy Thompson; Roger Walker; Michael Way; David Whately; and Neil Williamson. Not everyone was in agreement with my arguments and I alone am responsible for the views expressed. I am also most grateful to my agent Doreen Montgomery and publisher David Thomas who have guided me through writing my first book. Finally, the book would not have been possible without the painstaking help and encouragement of my wife Averil.

Bill Houston

Index

183

INDEX

INDEX

INDEX

Introducing No Surprises!

An executive report and board agenda to ensure that you and your business are not taken unawares by the last stages of the business cycle.

By March 1989 the USA was in the seventy-sixth month of the longest period of growth since 1848 – the previous longest period was in the 1920s. Then, as now, growth has only continued through the creation of excess credit; your task will be to steer your business through the period of credit failure that has inevitably ended each cycle. But this is no ordinary end-of-cycle phenomenon: the extension of credit is now the largest in history.

The aim of *Avoiding Adversity* is to take the reader through the essential stages of preparing a business for a major change in the credit cycle, without inflicting a painful operating contraction. Busy executives often do not have the time to consider the strategic implications of change, BUT NEITHER DO THEY WANT TO BE CAUGHT UNPREPARED.

The aim of No Surprises is to provide senior business executives with a regular report of leading indicators based on those provided in *Avoiding Adversity*. There will also be a briefing on the significant matters that should be included in the monthly board agenda.

The No Surprises team will consist of the author and senior business men on both sides of the Atlantic who will be available for private briefings, seminars, reports, and able to help with the preparation of alternative strategies. These plans are likely to cover:

- Significant methods of funding debt and reducing costs without imparing business operating effectiveness
- Methods of protecting the value of balance sheets in a regime of uncertainty and rising interest rates
- New investment opportunities that will arise

INTRODUCING NO SURPRISES!

- New methods of helping individuals become independent

If you wish to know more about No Surprises, please write to one of the following addresses, ensuring that you mention your company name and position:

Bill Houston
1325 Morris Drive,
Suite 201,
Wayne, PA 19087 – 5506

Brook Hunt & Associates Ltd
Old Bank House,
11 London Road,
Chertsey,
Surrey KT16 8AP.

ADVICE FROM THE TOP
Business Strategies of Britain's Corporate Leaders
Derek Ezra and David Oates

Derek Ezra introduces *Advice From The Top* in which twelve of our most distinguished internationally-renowned business leaders talk frankly about how they handle the key aspects of running a successful business: social responsibility, teamwork, delegation, strategic planning, and dealing with crises. Revealed here are the strategies and attitudes which have taken them to the top of their industries and have kept them there – in some cases for thirty years or more.

Corporate leadership has become a demanding way of life, calling for the rare and valued qualities of resilience and patience. Each of the contributors to this thought-provoking book has these qualities in abundance, and their experiences will be both a practical help and an inspiration to those who aspire to following in their footsteps.

The contributors are: Sir Adrian Cadbury; Sir Terence Conran; Sir John Cuckney; Sir Monty Finniston; Sir Robert Haslam; Sir Hector Laing; Sir Austin Pearce; Anita Roddick; Peter de Savary; Sir Adam Thomson; Sir Francis Tombs and Sir Graham Wilkins.

MAKING AN IMPACT
Harvey Thomas with Liz Gill

Do you have a speech to make or a TV interview to face, a company video to present, a press conference to handle or a campaign to organise? In short, do you have a message to get across? If you do, then this book will ensure that you get it across successfully.

Over the past thirty years Harvey Thomas has planned and staged thousands of conference and promotional events in more than ninety countries. He brought a new style of presentation to Conservative Party rallies at the 1979 General Election and has continued to mastermind Tory conference and election events, as well as coaching government ministers, public figures and top executives on the art of public speaking and self-presentation.

In *Making an Impact* Harvey Thomas brings his immensely successful techniques to a larger audience, giving advice on practically every aspect of public presentation, from the one-to-one interview to the complexities of the major conference. He also has a wealth of stories to tell, with fascinating insights into many famous people he has worked with.

For executives on every rung of the corporate ladder, for political campaigners, and anyone who wants their message to be heard, this book is essential reading.

THE 20% FACTOR
The Key to Personal and Corporate Success
Graham Lancaster

A must for all company libraries! *The 20% Factor* is the latest book from the chairman and chief executive of Biss Lancaster, a leading UK PR company which is part of one of the world's largest communications groups. Drawing on his experience as policy advisor to the CBI, Graham Lancaster claims that individuals can improve both their personal and corporate performance by twenty per cent almost immediately by taking some simple steps to understand and utilise image-making, establish good personal contacts and develop public relations.

Written in an intelligent and entertaining manner, the book uses a mixture of successful techniques to enable readers and their organisations to monitor their performance more effectively than ever before.

GETTING THROUGH
How to Make Words Work
Godfrey Howard

This is the book which brought together some of the most intelligent people in the world, when it was chosen as a theme for the international MENSA conference at Queen's College, Cambridge. In this remarkable rewrite the book now launches invaluable advice for communication into the 1990s.

This is what they said about the first edition:

'If you want to get a job interview, ask for a raise, propose marriage or seduction, write a compelling sales letter or create a great advertisement, read this book first. It will focus your mind wonderfully.'

Saatchi & Saatchi

'*Getting Through* is such an inspiration. Apart from practising what it teaches, recommending it at every lecture on communication and using it as a map, I have finally used it as a theme for the international MENSA conference . . . '

John McNulty, MENSA committee

'I find it fascinating. Every school leaver should buy a copy, read it – and give it to their parents.'

John Whitney, Director General, Independent Broadcasing Authority